Global History and Geography
Regents Test Prep Workbook

HOLT

WORLD HISTORY
Human Legacy
New York

HOLT, RINEHART AND WINSTON

A Harcourt Education Company

Orlando • Austin • New York • San Diego • London

Contributor and Reviewer

Jason E. Lyons
High School Teacher
North Collins Central School District
North Collins, New York

ISBN-13: 978-0-03-093849-8
ISBN 0-03-093849-X

1 2 3 4 5 6 7 8 9 912 12 11 10 09 08 07

Contents

To the Teacher

At the conclusion of the school year, your students will take the Regents High School Examination in Global History and Geography. To help you prepare your students for this exam, Holt Social Studies has created the *Global History and Geography Regents Prep Workbook*. Its pages include an instructional section with test-taking tips, scoring rubrics, and practice tests. When used in conjunction with *Holt Human Legacy, New York*, you can be certain that, come exam day, you will have prepared your students well for success on the exam.

Before assigning any of the practice tests, encourage your students to review the test-taking tips section found at the front of the book. These tips have been adapted from a series of strategies developed by Jason E. Lyons, a New York high school teacher, to prepare his students for taking the Regents exam. The test-taking tips instruct students on how best to approach the different types of questions that they will encounter on the exam. These tips also include strategies for eliminating incorrect answers in multiple-choice questions, using note-taking to decode document-based questions, and making mind maps to brainstorm essay responses. Practice questions are included along with the instructional material to reinforce learning as it occurs.

Also included in the front of the book are two generic scoring rubrics—one for thematic essays, and one for document-based essays. Careful review of these rubrics by your students will give them greater knowledge in answering the types of essay questions found on the Regents exam. The document-based essay rubric incorporates recent revisions to the scoring criteria for these items. The New York State Education Department has requested that Social Studies teachers be aware of these changes as they prepare students for the Regents exam.

Eight practice tests, each correlated to one of the eight units of study in of New York's Core Curriculum for Global History and Geography, comprise the remainder of the book's contents. These tests are also in alignment with the five New York State Social Studies Standards. Each practice test, called an activity, consists of three parts. Part I contains 20 multiple-choice questions that are designed to review course content while familiarizing students with the style of questions they will face on the Regents exam. Part II contains thematic essay questions. Part III contains seven primary and secondary source documents with short-answer questions. Each short-answer question builds towards the writing of a document-based essay.

Finally, for additional practice, the workbook concludes with the complete version of New York's August 2006 Regents High School Examination in Global History and Geography. Answers for all of these tests can be found in a separate answer key booklet.

As a student in New York, you will take the Regents High School Examination in Global History and Geography at the end of this school year. To help you prepare for the test, Holt Social Studies has created the *Global History and Geography Regents Prep Workbook.* Included in this book are test-taking tips, scoring information, practice tests, and a complete Regents exam. Completing these materials as assigned will help you to succeed on exam day.

Before doing any of the practice tests, take some time to go over the test-taking tips found at the front of the book. These pages review the format of the Regents High School Examination in United States History and Government. They also will teach you how to approach the different kinds of questions on the test. Completing the practice questions on these pages will help you to get the most from what you learn.

Also in the front of the book are two of what teachers call "scoring rubrics." A scoring rubric tells a teacher how to grade answers to questions that require a written response. After you take the Regents High School Examination in United States History and Government in the spring, people correcting your test will use a rubric to grade your written responses to test questions. Knowing how your answers will be graded should help you feel confident when you respond to these questions.

The rest of the book contains 8 practice tests, called activities. Each activity is divided into three parts. Part I contains 20 multiple-choice questions. These questions review what you have already learned in class, and will help you to remember the information that you will be expected to know for the test. Part II contains a thematic essay question. Part III is made up of seven documents, each followed by two or three questions. Answering these questions will help you write an essay, called a document-based essay, on a topic that will be given to you. Finally, for extra practice, a complete version of the August 2006 Regents High School Examination in Global History and Geography has been included at the end of this workbook.

Mastering Key Terms and People

Success on the Regents exam starts long before exam day. It starts with mastering the language of history and geography. This language is complex because it involves key terms as well as key players—those people whose actions have affected history and geography.

Building your knowledge of key terms and people will greatly improve your ability to access information in your textbook, participate in lessons, and succeed on the Regents exam. The best way to master this language is in the context of learning. Using the strategies below will help you to learn new terms as you encounter them.

KEY TERMS AND PEOPLE

Holt Human Legacy helps you build your vocabulary by highlighting key terms and people at the beginning of each section. You will encounter the definitions in section content Use this list to start your own list of key terms and people. Add to your list whenever you come across an unfamiliar term.

Key Terms	Key People
Renaissance humanism secular	Leonardo da Vinci Michelangelo Buonarroti Raphael

FLASH CARDS

Create flash cards to help you learn key terms and people from your list. Write each term on the front of an index card. On the back of the card, write the term's definition, a description, and important related details.

"rebirth"; an era following the Middle Ages; a movement that started in Italy and centered on the revival of interest in the classical learning of Greece and Rome

Leonardo da Vinci

- (1452–1519) Italian painter, sculptor, musician, engineer, and scientist
- associated with Italian Renaissance
- painted the *Mona Lisa* and *The Last Supper*

KNOW YOUR "–ISMS"

Pay careful attention to "**–isms**." Often, words ending in "–ism" express concepts that are key to the study of history and geography. These terms may express a doctrine, a process, a belief system, a theory, a philosophy, a social or political movement, or even a prejudice or bias.

As you read, make flash cards for all of the "–isms" that you encounter. Be sure to include the "–isms" listed in New York's Global History and Geography standards. These terms commonly appear on the Regents exam and include the following:

- Absolutism
- Animism
- Anti-Semitism
- Buddhism
- Capitalism
- Communism
- Confucianism
- Daoism
- Expansionism
- Fascism
- Feudalism
- Hinduism
- Humanism
- Imperialism
- Industrialism
- Islamic fundamentalism
- Jainism
- Judaism
- Legalism
- Manorialism
- Marxism
- Mercantilism
- Militarism
- Nationalism
- Pan-Africanism
- Post-colonialism
- Shintoism
- Social Darwinism
- Terrorism

Strategies for Multiple-Choice Questions

How can you become more skilled at answering multiple-choice questions? For starters, you need to know how these questions are structured. A multiple-choice question consists of a single stem and several answer options. The stem can be either a question or an incomplete sentence. Four answer options usually appear below the stem. These options can answer the question or complete the sentence. Only one option is the best answer. The other options, called distracters, are incorrect.

Using the following strategies will help you correctly answer multiple-choice questions. The sample questions have been adapted from the January 2006 Global History and Geography Regents Exam.

LEARN
STEP 1: Read the Question

❶ Read the stem carefully. Determine whether it is a question or an incomplete sentence.

❷ Highlight key words and facts in the stem. They may help you determine the correct answer.

STEP 2: Take Notes in the Margin

❸ Take notes in the margin to help you understand what the question is really asking.

- The question has to do with where people live.
- They are all landforms.

❸

DIRECTIONS Read each question and circle the number of the best response.

1 What was one effect of Alexander the Great's conquests? ❶
   (1) expansion of Hellenistic culture
   (2) decline of Hellenistic culture
   (3) decreased importance of the Silk Roads
   (4) increased support of the Mayan leaders

Base your answer to question 2 on the statement below and on your knowledge of social studies. ❷

Throughout history, people have lived in savannas, in deserts, on mountains, in river valleys, along coastlines, and on islands.

2 This statement demonstrates that people
   (1) adapt to their surroundings.
   (2) develop a common language.
   (3) organize similar forms of government.
   (4) prefer to live only in isolated areas.

Answer Options

LEARN
STEP 3: Eliminate Incorrect Answers

4 Eliminate answer options that you know are incorrect.

5 If two answer options disagree with each other, one of them is likely to be the correct answer.

6 Watch for words such as *always*, *only*, and *never*. Answer options that include these words are often incorrect. These words indicate that the correct answer must be an undisputed fact. In social studies, few facts are undisputed.

DIRECTIONS Read each question and circle the number of the best response.

1 What was one effect of Alexander the Great's conquests?
   (1) expansion of Hellenistic culture
   (2) decline of Hellenistic culture
   (3) decreased importance of the Silk Roads
   (4) increased support of the Mayan leaders

Base your answer to question 2 on the statement below and on your knowledge of social studies.

Throughout history, people have lived in savannas, in deserts, on mountains, in river valleys, along coastlines, and on islands.

2 This statement demonstrates that people
   (1) adapt to their surroundings.
   (2) develop a common language.
   (3) organize similar forms of government.
   (4) prefer to live only in isolated areas.

LEARN
STEP 4: Review and Answer

❼ Re-read the question.

❽ Consider the options that remain and select the best answer choice. If you are not sure of the answer, select the option that makes the most sense.

DIRECTIONS Read each question and circle the number of the best response.

1 What was one effect of Alexander the Great's conquests?
(1) expansion of Hellenistic culture
(2) decline of Hellenistic culture
(3) decreased importance of the Silk Roads
(4) increased support of the Mayan leaders

Base your answer to question 2 on the statement below and on your knowledge of social studies.

Throughout history, people have lived in savannas, in deserts, on mountains, in river valleys, along coastlines, and on islands.

2 This statement demonstrates that people
❽ (1) adapt to their surroundings.
(2) develop a common language.
(3) organize similar forms of government.
(4) prefer to live only in isolated areas.

Practice

DIRECTIONS Read each question and circle the number of the best response.

1   Although South Africa was granted independence in 1910, under apartheid,

    (1) black South Africans placed restrictions on white-owned businesses.

    (2) black South Africans were denied citizenship.

    (3) black and white South Africans both ran for political office.

    (4) the larger black population had the best farmland.

2   How was the Vietnam War related to the domino theory?

    (1) Vietnam had built up its military and planned to invade Cambodia and Thailand.

    (2) The Soviet Union invaded China to prevent it from attacking Vietnam.

    (3) The United States did not want a Communist government to take control of Vietnam.

    (4) France agreed to allow Vietnam to set up a democracy to stop the spread of communism.

3   How did the Iranian Revolution change Iran?

    (1) A conservative religious government came to power.

    (2) Iran established better relations with the West.

    (3) Women gained more power in government.

    (4) Iran became a Communist country.

4   Which of the following is a characteristic of a developing nation?

    (1) widespread technology

    (2) inadequate education

    (3) a broad health care system

    (4) an economy based on manufacturing

5   How is globalization changing the world?

    (1) It is eliminating poverty in many countries.

    (2) It is linking countries through trade and culture.

    (3) It is reducing economic interdependence.

    (4) It is eliminating free trade.

Practice Answers: 1. (2); 2. (3); 3. (1); 4. (2); 5. (2)

Strategies for Thematic Essay Questions

Thematic essay questions test your knowledge of large-scale events and trends in global history and geography. First, you will be given a broad theme. Then, you will be given a task that asks you to think of specific things, events, or actions that exemplify the theme. Finally, you will write an essay telling how the things, actions, or events fit into the larger historical picture. You will be given suggestions about which things, actions, or events you might want to include. You do not have to follow the suggestions. The sample question has been adapted from the June 2006 Regents exam. Use these strategies to write your thematic essay:

STUDY THE QUESTION

❶ Carefully read the *Theme* to understand the topic of the essay you will be asked to write.

❷ The information in this box provides more information about the theme.

❸ The *Task* gives specific details about the topic of the essay and instructions for writing.

❹ A list of suggested examples of things, events, or people follows the *Task*.

❺ These guidelines will help you organize your essay.

THEMATIC ESSAY QUESTION

❶ **THEME** Conflict

❷ | Conflicts between groups of people have threatened peace in many nations and regions. |

TASK Identify one conflict that has threatened peace in a nation or region and

❸
- Discuss **one** major cause of that conflict.
- Identify **two** groups involved in the conflict and discuss **one** viewpoint of **each** group.
- Discuss the extent to which the conflict was *or* was *not* resolved.

❹ You may use any major conflict from your study of global history. Some suggestions you might wish to consider include the Crusades, the French Revolution, World War I, the Russian Revolution, the Chinese Civil War, the policy of apartheid in South Africa, the Rwandan Civil War, and the Bosnian War.

Do *not* use conflicts that *occurred* in the United States in your answer.

You are *not* limited to these suggestions.

❺ **GUIDELINES**

In your essay, be sure to

- Develop all aspects of the task
- Support the theme with relevant facts, examples, and details
- Use a logical and clear plan of organization, including an introduction and a conclusion that are beyond a restatement of the theme

MIND-MAPPING

❶ Brainstorm ideas for your essay using a mind map like the one below. A mind map will help you to organize information, make connections between ideas and facts, and structure your essay.

❷ Write the *Theme* in the center of your mind map. Typically, main ideas and core concepts are at the center of mind maps. Keep in mind that you will develop the introductory paragraph of your essay based on the *Theme*.

❸ Make one arm for each piece of information outlined in the *Task*. These arms represent supporting details and ideas. Draw connecting lines between main ideas and supporting details to show how ideas are related.

❹ Add any additional information or supporting details that you think are important.

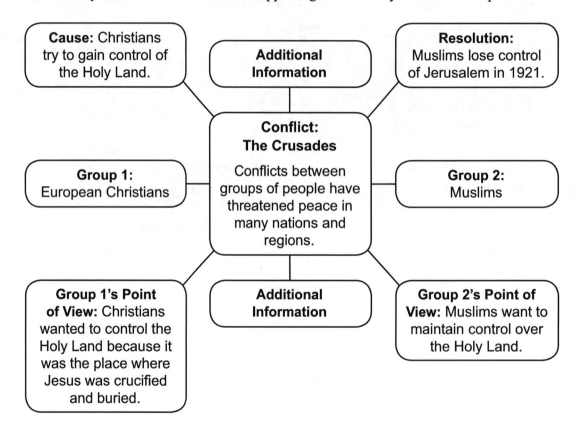

WRITE YOUR ESSAY

Follow these steps to write your thematic essay:

STEP ❶ Use the mind map you created to write a draft of your essay. Before you start writing, make sure that you have filled out your mind map with enough information to answer all of the questions in the *Task* box.

STEP ❷ Write an introduction based on the *Theme* and *Task*. Develop a thesis statement, a statement telling what your essay will be about, based on information from the center box of your mind map. Be sure to include specific information about your topic. Be careful not to just copy the information provided in the question.

STEP ❸ Write supporting paragraphs based on the topics in each arm of your mind map. Begin with a sentence that links your paragraph's topic to your introduction. Then, tell about the thing, event, or person. Give as many specific details as you can, such as the dates and places of the events or situations that you describe. Be sure to cover all of the bulleted points in the *Task* box.

STEP ❹ Write a conclusion for your essay. Make sure that you restate your thesis and have summarized ideas and information from the body of your essay.

STEP ❺ Evaluate and revise your essay. Review your essay to make sure that you have covered all of the bulleted points in the *Task* box. Then, look closely at each paragraph. Revise wording or sentence structure to strengthen links between main ideas and details. Lastly, double-check the spelling of all names of people, places, and events.

Practice

The following practice question has been adapted from the January 2006 Regents Exam for Global History and Geography.

Answers to the essay questions are to be written in the separate essay booklet.

In developing your answer, be sure to keep these general definitions in mind:

    (a) *Explain* **means "to make plain or understandable; to give reasons for or causes of; to show the logical development or relationships of."**

    (b) *Discuss* **means "to make observations about something using facts, reasoning, and argument; to present in some detail."**

THEME Change

> The ideas and beliefs of philosophers and leaders have led to changes in nations and regions.

TASK Choose *two* philosophers *and/or* leaders and for *each*

> - Explain a major idea or belief of that philosopher or leader
> - Discuss how that idea or belief changed one nation or region

You may use any philosophers or leaders from your study of global history. Some suggestions you might wish to consider include Confucius, John Locke, Adam Smith, Simón Bolívar, Otto von Bismarck, Vladimir Lenin, Mohandas Gandhi, Mao Zedong, Fidel Castro, and Nelson Mandela.

Do *not* use a philosopher or leader from the United States in your answer.

You are *not* limited to these suggestions.

GUIDELINES

In your essay, be sure to:

- develop all aspects of the task
- support the theme with relevant facts, examples, and details
- use a logical and clear plan of organization, including an introduction and a conclusion that are beyond a restatement of the theme

Strategies for Document-Based Questions

For the document-based questions, you will be asked to analyze a series of eight written and visual documents. These documents may include excerpts from texts, quotations, maps, charts, graphs, time lines, photographs, and political cartoons. You will answer one or more short-answer questions for each document. Then, you will be asked to use the documents and your answers to the short-answers questions to write a document-based essay on a certain topic. Use the strategies below to answer document-based questions. The sample questions have been adapted from the June 2006 Regents exam for Global History and Geography.

LEARN

❶ Carefully read the background information on the subject of the documents that you will be analyzing.

❷ The *Task* describes the steps you will follow to complete this part of the exam.

❸ To analyze visual documents, determine the type of visual that is shown and when it was created.

❹ Identify who or what is portrayed in the visual. Look for details, and note how the subject is depicted. Ask yourself whether the visual agrees with what you know about the period.

Part A: Short-Answer Questions

❶ HISTORICAL CONTEXT The Industrial Revolution that began in Europe changed American society in many ways. Some of these changes were positive while others were negative.

❷ TASK Using information from the documents and your knowledge of global history, answer the questions that follow each document in Part A. Your answers to the questions will help you write the Part B essay in which you will be asked to

DIRECTIONS Discuss both the positive and the negative effects of the Industrial Revolution on American society.

DOCUMENT 1
Child Labor in New York City, c. 1880s

❸
❹

© Bettmann/CORBIS

1. What does this photograph suggest about working conditions during the Industrial Revolution?

The photograph suggests that working conditions

were poor and that children sometimes worked.

LEARN *(continued)*

5 Begin analyzing a written document by finding it's source. Ask yourself who the author of the document is. When was the document created?

6 Read the document. Read the entire document from start to finish. Then, read the document again and take notes in the margin.

7 Highlight important words. Isolating key terms will help you make sense of the document.

8 Read the short-answer questions. Expect to re-read the document several times. Use your notes to help you answer each question. Always use complete sentences.

9 Check your work. Make sure that you have included all of the information that you want. Think about how each document might help you write the essay to come.

DOCUMENT 2

6 The early millgirls were of different ages. Some were not over ten years old; a few were in middle life, but the majority were between the ages of sixteen and twenty-five . . .

7 The most prevailing incentive to labor was to secure the means of education for some male member of the family. To make a gentleman of a brother or a son, to give him a college education, was the dominant thought in the minds of a great many of the better class of millgirls. I have known more than one to give every cent of her wages, month after month, to her brother, that he might get the education necessary to enter some profession.

—Harriet Robinson, former millworker, "Early Factory Labor in New England," 1883

8 2. What was the most prevailing incentive for the girls to work?

9 *Girls worked to help pay for the education of one*

of their male family members.

LEARN

10 The document-based activity concludes with an essay that requires you to use information from the documents and your knowledge of history.

11 Carefully read the *Task* for the essay topic and specific instructions for writing your essay.

12 These Guidelines will help you organize your essay.

10 Part B: Document-Based Essay

HISTORICAL CONTEXT The Industrial Revolution that began in Europe changed American society in many ways. Some of these changes were positive while others were negative.

11 **TASK** Using information from the documents and your knowledge of global history, write an essay in which you

- Discuss both the positive **and** the negative effects of the Industrial Revolution on American society.

DIRECTIONS Using the information from the documents and your knowledge of global history, write a well-organized essay that includes an introduction, several paragraphs, and a conclusion. Use evidence from at least *five* documents in your essay. Support your response with relevant facts, examples, and details. Include additional outside information.

12 GUIDELINES

In your essay, be sure to:

- Develop all aspects of the task
- Incorporate information from at least *five* documents
- Incorporate relevant outside information
- Support the theme with relevant facts, examples, and details
- Use a logical and clear plan of organization, including an introduction and a conclusion that are beyond a restatement of the theme

Using Mind-Maps for Document-Based Essays

Mind-mapping is one of the most effective prewriting techniques for writing document-based essays. Using a mind map will help you organize and prioritize information. Follow these steps to make a mind map for a document-based essay.

STEP ❶ Write the *Task* in the center of your mind map. As you fill out your graph, keep in that the *Task* will be the basis for the introduction to your document-based essay.

STEP ❷ Use links from the center to connect the *Task* to the documents. Create one arm for each document. Draw connecting lines between main ideas and supporting details to show how ideas are related.

STEP ❸ Use your answers from the short-answer section to fill out details about each document. Add any additional outside information that you think is relevant. Helpful hint: Scan the multiple-choice section for relevant details and information to use in your essay.

STEP ❹ Develop an outline and a rough draft of your essay based on your mind map. Be sure to set aside time to revise and make corrections to your essay before turning in your exam.

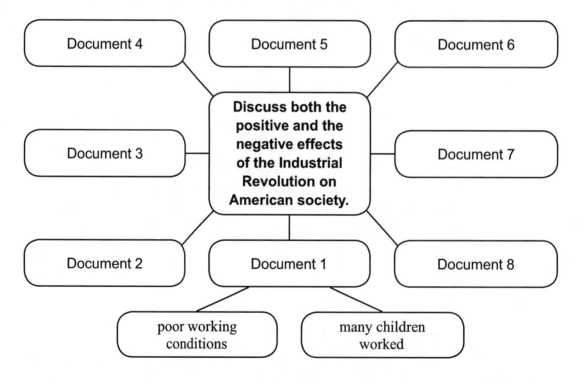

Practice

The following practice questions have been adapted from the January 2006 Regents Exam for Global History and Geography.

Part A: Short-Answer Questions

HISTORICAL CONTEXT In the late 1800s and early 1900s, imperialism affected many societies throughout the world. Perspectives on imperialism differed depending on a person's point of view.

TASK Using the information from the documents and your knowledge of global history, answer the questions that follow each document in Part A. Your answers to the questions will help you to write the Part B essay.

DIRECTIONS Examine the following documents and answer the short-answer questions that follow each document.

DOCUMENT 1

> . . . The value of the Industrial mission, on the other hand, depends, of course, largely on the nature of the tribes among whom it is located. Its value can hardly be over-estimated among such people as the Waganda, both on account of their natural aptitude and their eager desire to learn. But even the less advanced and more primitive tribes may be equally benefited, if not only mechanical and artisan work, such as the carpenter's and blacksmith's craft, but also the simpler expedients [ways] of agriculture are taught. The sinking of wells, the system of irrigation, the introduction and planting of useful trees, the use of manure, and of domestic animals for agricultural purposes, the improvement of his implements [tools] by the introduction of the primitive Indian plough, etc. — all of these, while improving the status of the native, will render [make] his land more productive, and hence, by increasing his surplus products, will enable him to purchase from the trader the cloth which shall add to his decency, and the implements and household utensils which shall produce greater results for his labour and greater comforts in his social life. . .
>
> —Frederick D. Lugard, from *The Rise of Our East African Empire*, 1893

1. Based on this document, state two ways the author thinks British imperialism would benefit Africans.

_____

_____

_____

DOCUMENT 2

> Thus all the imperialists, without exception, evolved the means, their colonial policies, to satisfy the ends, the exploitation of the subject territories for the aggrandizement [enhancement] of the metropolitan [imperialistic] countries. They were all rapacious [greedy]; they all subserved the needs of the subject lands to their own demands; they all circumscribed [limited] human rights and liberties; they all repressed and despoiled, degraded and oppressed. They took our lands, our lives, our resources, and our dignity. Without exception, they left us nothing but our resentment, and later, our determination to be free and rise once more . . .
>
> —Kwame Nkrumah from *Africa Must Unite*, 1970

2. According to the document, what is one criticism made about the European imperialists?

_____

_____

Part B: Document-Based Essay

HISTORICAL CONTEXT In the late 1800s and early 1900s, imperialism affected many societies throughout the world. Perspectives on imperialism differed depending on a person's point of view.

TASK Using the information from the documents and your knowledge of global history, write an essay in which you

- Discuss imperialism from the point of view of the imperialist power
- Discuss imperialism from the point of view of the colonized people

DIRECTIONS Write a well-organized essay that includes an introduction, several paragraphs, and a conclusion. Use evidence from at least *five* documents in your essay. Support your response with relevant facts, examples, and details. Include additional outside information.

GUIDELINES
In your essay, be sure to:

- Develop all aspects of the task
- Incorporate information from at least *five* documents
- Incorporate relevant outside information
- Support the theme with relevant facts, examples, and details
- Use a logical and clear plan of organization, including an introduction and a conclusion that are beyond a restatement of the theme

Thematic Essays

Score of 5:

- Thoroughly develops all aspects of the task evenly and in depth
- Is more analytical than descriptive (analyzes, evaluates, and /or creates information)
- Richly supports the theme with many relevant facts, examples, and details
- Demonstrates a logical and clear plan of organization; includes an introduction and a conclusion that are beyond a restatement of the theme

Score of 4:

- Develops all aspects of the task but may do so somewhat unevenly
- Is both descriptive and analytical (applies, analyzes, evaluates, and/or creates information)
- Supports the theme with relevant facts, examples, and details
- Demonstrates a logical and clear plan of organization; includes an introduction and a conclusion that are beyond a restatement of the theme

Score of 3:

- Develops all aspects of the task with little depth or develops most aspects of the task in some depth
- Is more descriptive than analytical (applies, may analyze, and/or may evaluate information)
- Includes some relevant facts, examples, and details; may include some minor inaccuracies
- Demonstrates a satisfactory plan of organization; includes an introduction and a conclusion that may be a restatement of the theme

Score of 2:

- Minimally develops all aspects of the task or develops some aspects of the task in some depth
- Is primarily descriptive; may include faulty, weak, or isolated application or analysis
- Includes few relevant facts, examples, and details; may include some inaccuracies
- Demonstrates a general plan of organization; may lack focus; may contain digressions; may not clearly identify which aspect of the task is being addressed; may lack an introduction and/or a conclusion

Score of 1:

- Minimally develops some aspects of the task
- Is descriptive; may lack understanding, application, or analysis
- Includes few relevant facts, examples, or details; may include inaccuracies
- May demonstrate a weakness in organization; may lack focus; may contain digressions; may not clearly identify which aspect of the task is being addressed; may lack an introduction and/or a conclusion

Score of 0:

- Fails to develop the task or may only refer to the theme in a general way; *OR* includes no relevant facts, examples, or details; *OR* includes only the theme, task, or suggestions as copied from the test booklet; *OR* is illegible; *OR* is a blank paper

Document-Based Essays

Score of 5:

- Thoroughly develops all aspects of the task evenly and in depth
- Is more analytical than descriptive (analyzes, evaluates, and /or creates information)
- Incorporates relevant information from at least four documents
- Incorporates substantial relevant outside information
- Richly supports the theme with many relevant facts, examples, and details
- Demonstrates a logical and clear plan of organization; includes an introduction and a conclusion that are beyond a restatement of the theme

Score of 4:

- Develops all aspects of the task but may do so somewhat unevenly
- Is both descriptive and analytical (applies, analyzes, evaluates, and/or creates information)
- Incorporates relevant information from at least four documents
- Incorporates relevant outside information
- Supports the theme with relevant facts, examples, and details
- Demonstrates a logical and clear plan of organization; includes an introduction and a conclusion that are beyond a restatement of the theme

Score of 3:

- Develops all aspects of the task with little depth or develops most aspects of the task in some depth
- Is more descriptive than analytical (applies, may analyze, and/or may evaluate information)
- Incorporates some relevant information from some of the documents
- Incorporates limited relevant outside information
- Includes some relevant facts, examples, and details; may include some minor inaccuracies
- Demonstrates a satisfactory plan of organization; includes an introduction and a conclusion that may be a restatement of the theme

Score of 2:

- Minimally develops all aspects of the task or develops some aspects of the task in some depth
- Is primarily descriptive; may include faulty, weak, or isolated application or analysis
- Incorporates limited relevant information from the documents or consists primarily of relevant information copied from the documents
- Presents little or no relevant outside information
- Includes few relevant facts, examples, and details; may include some inaccuracies
- Demonstrates a general plan of organization; may lack focus; may contain digressions; may not clearly identify which aspect of the task is being addressed; may lack an introduction and/or a conclusion

Score of 1:

- Minimally develops some aspects of the task
- Is descriptive; may lack understanding, application, or analysis
- Makes vague, unclear references to the documents or consists primarily of relevant and irrelevant information copied from the documents

- Presents no relevant outside information

- Includes few relevant facts, examples, or details; may include inaccuracies

- May demonstrate a weakness in organization; may lack focus; may contain digressions; may not clearly identify which aspect of the task is being addressed; may lack an introduction and/or a conclusion

Score of 0:

- Fails to develop the task or may only refer to the theme in a general way; *OR* includes no relevant facts, examples, or details; *OR* includes only the historical context and/or task as copied from the test booklet; *OR* includes only entire documents copied from the test booklet; *OR* is illegible; *OR* is a blank paper

Activity 1   Part I: Multiple-Choice Questions
Ancient World—Civilizations and Religions

DIRECTIONS Read each question and circle the number of the best response.

Base your answer to question 1 on the map below and on your knowledge of social studies.

Ancient India, c. 500 BC

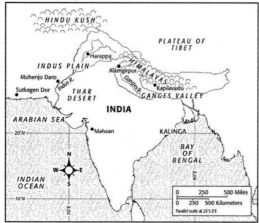

1   On which river did the ancient Indian city of Mohenjo Daro develop?

   (1) Ganges
   (2) Indus
   (3) Kalinga
   (4) Hyphasis

2   What technological innovation resulted in the Neolithic Revolution?

   (1) the ability to make fire
   (2) domestication of plants
   (3) development of writing systems
   (4) development of stone tools

3   The development of Christianity was most influenced by which other major world religion?

   (1) Islam
   (2) Hinduism
   (3) Buddhism
   (4) Judaism

4   The golden age of Greek philosophy was inspired by Socrates, Plato, and

   (1) Augustus Caesar
   (2) Alexander the Great
   (3) Aristotle
   (4) Homer

5   The Mandate of Heaven is a Chinese concept used to explain the

   (1) balancing of natural forces
   (2) rise of democracy
   (3) rise and fall of dynasties
   (4) flooding of the Huang River

Activity 1   Part I: Multiple-Choice Questions

Ancient World—Civilizations and Religions

Base your answer to question 6 on the passage below and on your knowledge of social studies.

> 196. If a man put out the eye of another man, his eye shall be put out.
>
> 198. If he put out the eye of a freed man . . . he shall pay one gold mina.
>
> 199. If he put out the eye of a man's slave . . . he shall pay one-half of its value.
>
> —from Hammurabi's Code

6   According to this passage from Hammurabi's Code, in Babylonian society
   (1) women and men were treated equally under the law
   (2) slavery was illegal
   (3) slaves could not be freed
   (4) punishment depended on a person's social class

7   In which type of environment did the first civilizations develop?
   (1) islands
   (2) mountain ranges
   (3) deserts
   (4) river valleys

8   The ancient Egyptians' system of writing was based on
   (1) abstract symbols
   (2) picture symbols
   (3) knotted strings of various colors
   (4) the lunar calendar

9   Which event in the history of ancient Indian civilization occurred first?
   (1) founding of Buddhism
   (2) development of the caste system
   (3) writing of the Vedas
   (4) the rise of Mohenjo Daro

10   The Stone Age is divided into periods based on
   (1) migration patterns
   (2) climate features
   (3) advances in toolmaking
   (4) advances in belief systems

11   The domestication of maize most contributed to development of civilizations in
   (1) the Indus River valley
   (2) South America
   (3) the Fertile Crescent
   (4) Mesoamerica

12 Social classes in early civilizations were often based on

(1) beliefs
(2) family ties
(3) individual merit
(4) a person's place of birth

13 Which of the following would most likely lead to the process of cultural diffusion?

(1) geographic isolation
(2) long-distance trade
(3) stone tools
(4) suspicion of foreigners

14 The geography of Mesopotamia led people to

(1) migrate to the Indus River valley
(2) adopt hunting and gathering as a permanent way of life
(3) develop large irrigation projects
(4) build along the Mediterranean coastline

15 Which of the following helped early villages become cities?

(1) increased food production
(2) advances in record keeping
(3) creation of legal codes
(4) development of religions

Base your answer to question 16 on the graphic organizer below and on your knowledge of social studies.

16 Which effect best completes the cause-and-effect chart above?

(1) Hinduism develops in India.
(2) Chinese silk loses value.
(3) Chinese peasants gain social status.
(4) Buddhism spreads to China.

Activity 1

Part I: Multiple-Choice Questions

Ancient World—Civilizations and Religions

17 One factor that contributed to both the fall of the Roman Empire and the fall of China's Han dynasty was

(1) conquest by the Persians
(2) invasion by nomadic tribes
(3) spread of Islam
(4) invention of bronze weapons

18 The Pax Romana refers to the period when Rome had which of the following types of government?

(1) city-state
(2) empire
(3) republic
(4) democracy

19 Which type of belief system was most prevalent in Africa during the time of the Neolithic Revolution?

(1) animism
(2) Islam
(3) Legalism
(4) Christianity

20 In the Hellenistic world the city-state was replaced as the main political unit by the

(1) manor
(2) kingdom
(3) dynasty
(4) senate

Activity 1 | Part II: Thematic Essay

Ancient World—Civilizations and Religions

Answers to the essay questions are to be written on a separate sheet of paper.

In developing your answer to Part II, be sure to keep these general definitions in mind:

(a) *Describe* means "to tell about or to illustrate something in words."

(b) *Explain* means "to make plain or understandable; to give reasons for or causes of; to show the logical development or relationships of."

PART II: THEMATIC ESSAY QUESTION

DIRECTIONS Write a well-organized essay that includes an introduction, several paragraphs addressing the task below, and a conclusion.

THEME Political Systems

> Classical civilizations created political systems that continue to have an important influence today. Two examples of their influence include democracy and the republican form of government.

TASK Describe how the Greek city-state of Athens contributed to the development of democracy and how ancient Rome's government contributed to the development of the republican form of government. For *each* ancient civilization

> • Describe the structure of its government.
> • Explain how its government reflected the principle of democracy or the republican form of government.
> • Explain how its form of government influenced the development of the US political system.

You may use any example from your study of government in ancient Greece and Rome. Some suggestions you might wish to consider include voting, representation, the legislative branch, and popular sovereignty.

You are *not* limited to these suggestions.

GUIDELINES

In your essay, be sure to

- Develop all aspects of the task.

- Support the theme with relevant facts, examples, and details.

- Use a logical and clear plan of organization, including an introduction and a conclusion that are beyond a restatement of the theme.

Activity 1   Part III: Document-Based Activity

Ancient World—Civilizations and Religion

Part A: Using Source Materials

HISTORICAL CONTEXT Thousands of years ago the introduction of farming brought dramatic changes to peoples in many parts of the world. The development of agriculture led to the establishment of permanent settlements, which grew into towns and cities. In certain regions of the world, these towns and cities eventually blossomed into complex civilizations, like those in Mesopotamia, Egypt, India, and China. Each of these civilizations developed advanced technology to improve life for the people who lived there.

TASK Using information from the documents and your knowledge of world history, answer the questions that follow each document in Part A. Your answers to the questions will help you write the Part B essay.

DIRECTIONS Examine the following documents and answer the questions that follow each document.

DOCUMENT 1

> To the King my lord, thy servant Arad-Nana . . .
>
> To reduce the general inflammation of his [the patient's] forehead I tied a bandage upon it. His face is swollen. Yesterday as formerly I opened the wound which had been received in the midst of it. As for the bandage which was over the swelling, matter was upon the bandage the size of the tip of the little finger. Thy gods, if they can restore unto him the whole flesh of his body, cause thou to invoke, and his mouth will cry; "Peace forever! May the heart of the king my lord be good!" He will live seven or eight days.
>
> —letter from an Assyrian physician, c. 600s BC

1. What type of technology is discussed in this letter?

_____

_____

2. How might this technology have affected life in Assyria?

_____

_____

Activity 1

Part III: Document-Based Activity

Ancient World—Civilizations and Religion

DOCUMENT 2

**Detail from the Egyptian Book of the Dead
painting on papyrus, c. 1069–945 BC**

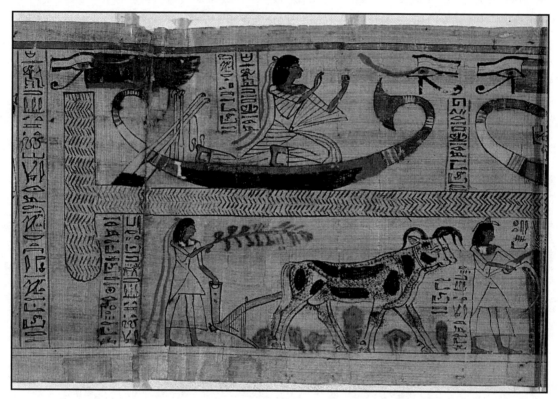

Detail from the Book of the Dead of the priest Aha-Mer depicting a barque and a farming scene,
Third Intermediate Period (papyrus), Egyptian, 21st Dynasty (c. 1069-945 BC / Egyptian
Museum, Turin, Italy, Alinari / The Bridgeman Art Library

3. What elements of Egyptian technology are depicted in the painting above?

_____

_____

4. How might those elements of technology have affected daily life in Egypt?

_____

_____

_____

Activity 1

Part III: Document-Based Activity

Ancient World—Civilizations and Religion

DOCUMENT 3

Before You Read The following words in the document below may be
new to you: *ramparts*, *bitumen*, *dikes*, *scarp*. You may want to look them
up in a dictionary.

> Nabupolassar, king of Babylon, the father that begat me, had made but had
> not finished the work of [building the great ramparts of Babylon]. The
> moat he had dug, and the two strong walls with bitumen and burnt brick
> had constructed along its bank: the dikes . . . he had made and a fence of
> burnt brick on the other side of the Euphrates: but he had not finished the
> rest . . . As for me, his eldest son, the beloved of his heart, I finished these
> great ramparts of Babylon. Beside the scarp of its moat the two strong
> walls with bitumen and burnt brick I built, and with the wall which my
> father had constructed I joined them, and the city, for cover, I carried them
> round . . .
>
> —inscription of Nebuchadnezzar, c. 604–561 BC

5. What construction projects were completed in Babylon during Nebuchadnezzar's
   reign?

   _____

   _____

   _____

6. What types of technology would have been necessary to complete these construction
   projects?

   _____

   _____

   _____

DOCUMENT 4

After this, they [the embalmers] fill the corpse's belly with crushed myrrh and cassia and other perfumed spices (but not with frankincense) and sew it back up. The next phase is to pack the corpse in natron [a type of salt] and leave it to mummify for seventy days—but they are not supposed to leave it for longer. Once the seventy days are over, they wash the corpse and then wrap the whole of its body in bandages made out of fine linen cloth cut into strips. The bandages have gum (which is usually used in Egypt instead of glue) smeared on their underside. Then the relatives come and collect the corpse. They make a hollow casket in the shape of a man and enclose the corpse inside it. Once the corpse has been shut away inside the casket, they store it upright against the wall in a burial chamber.

—Herodotus, *The Histories*, c. 440 BC

7. What practice does the document above describe? What types of knowledge would have likely been necessary in order to develop this practice?

_____

_____

_____

8. What role did the practice described above play in Egyptian life?

_____

_____

_____

Activity 1   Part III: Document-Based Activity
_____
Ancient World—Civilizations and Religion

DOCUMENT 5

Before You Read The following words in the document below may be
new to you: *attain, dichotomy*. You may want to look them up in a
dictionary.

There can no longer be any doubt that it was in China that the art of bronze
was born. It only took the ancient Chinese a few centuries to attain the
highest degree of mastery in the art, as proved by the pieces found at
Anyang; this suggests that the beginnings of the Bronze Age may perhaps
have coincided with those of the Shang dynasty . . . Bronze-casting brought
with it on the one hand a number of highly important technical innovations
such as horse-drawn chariots, writing, calendars, and new architectural
forms, and, on the other, a social dichotomy that was to be of vital
importance for Chinese history, by which society was divided into
townsfolk (warrior noblemen and hunters) and the peasantry.

—Jacques Gernet, *Ancient China:*
From Beginnings to the Empire, 1964

From "The Archaic Period" from *Ancient China: From the Beginnings to the Empire* by Jacques
Gernet, translated from the French by Raymond Rudorff. Copyright © 1964 by Presses
Universitaires de France, this translation copyright © 1968 by **Faber and Faber Ltd**.
Reproduced by permission of the publisher.

9. How did bronze-casting affect life in ancient China?

_____

_____

_____

10. How might bronze-casting have made life easier for the ancient Chinese?

_____

_____

_____

DOCUMENT 6

The most wonderful aspect of the Indus civilization was the excellent town-planning. The Indus civilization was an urban civilization and Mohenjo-daro was the oldest planned city of the world. Both the cities were populous and materially prosperous. The excellent town-planning is in itself a puzzling novelty. The buildings were of baked bricks, some two-storied and some even three-storied. The houses were in one line and the roads and lanes covered the space between the houses. Each house had a yard and was encircled with walls . . . The roads were wide and straight and there was a proper drainage system. The streets were from the north to the south so that the air could work as a sort of suction pump, thereby clearing the atmosphere automatically . . .

The excellent drainage system is most attractive. The drains led from individual houses to the back streets and from the back streets by cross drains to the main roads along which many deep drains ran out of the city.

—Arun Bhattacharjee, *History of Ancient India*, 1979

From "City Planning" from *History of Ancient India* by Arun Bhattacharjee. Copyright © 1979 by Arun Bhattacharjee. Reproduced by permission of **Sterling Publishers PVT. LTD.**

11. According to the document, what advanced technologies did the people of ancient India practice?

_____

_____

12. How might these technologies have influenced life in the Indus civilization?

_____

_____

_____

Part III: Document-Based Activity

Ancient World—Civilizations and Religion

DOCUMENT 7

Before You Read The following words in the document below may be new to you: *sericulture, rearing*. You may want to look them up in a dictionary.

> Sericulture was already highly developed as early as the 14th century BC, so that the Chinese must have begun rearing silkworms long before that time. On many bronze articles of the Shang Dynasty (c. 16th–11th century BC) are impressions of silk fabrics or fragments of spun silk. Silk-weaving technique was obviously already quite advanced at that time. A host of facts show that silk articles were becoming increasingly important in the social and economic life of the time, and that they had become media for the exchange of goods. The ensuing demand for silk fabrics led necessarily to the development of silkworm-raising in order to provide more and more raw material . . .
>
> In the Zhou Dynasty (c. 11th century–221 BC) cultivation of mulberry trees and rearing of silkworms flourished widely in both north and south China. Silk was the main material used in clothing the ruling class. Silk production from worm to fabric was women's chief productive activity.
>
> —Wang Zichun, from *Ancient China's Technology and Science*, 1983

From "Sericulture" by Wang Zichun from *China Knowledge Series: Ancient China's Technology and Science*, compiled by the *Institute of the History of Natural Sciences, Chinese Academy of Sciences*. Copyright © 1983 by Wang Zichun. Reproduced by permission of **Foreign Languages Press**.

13. According to the author, when did sericulture in China begin?

_____

_____

_____

14. For what was silk used in ancient China?

_____

_____

_____

Activity 1   Part III: Document-Based Activity
Ancient World—Civilizations and Religion

Part B: Writing a Document-Based Essay

HISTORICAL CONTEXT Thousands of years ago the introduction of farming brought dramatic changes to peoples in many parts of the world. The development of agriculture led to the establishment of permanent settlements, which grew into towns and cities. In certain regions of the world, these towns and cities eventually blossomed into complex civilizations, like those in Mesopotamia, Egypt, India, and China. Each of these civilizations developed advanced technology to improve life for the people who lived there.

TASK Using information from the documents and your knowledge of world history, write an essay in which you:

- Examine the accomplishments of the early river valley civilizations.

- Discuss how those accomplishments affected life in each civilization.

DIRECTIONS Using the information from the documents provided and your knowledge of world history, write a well-organized essay that includes an introduction, a body of several paragraphs, and a conclusion. In the body of the essay, use examples from at least *five* documents. Support your response with relevant facts, examples, and details. Include additional outside information.

GUIDELINES
In your essay, be sure to:

- Address all aspects of the **Task** by accurately analyzing and interpreting at least *five* documents.

- Incorporate information from the documents in the body of the essay.

- Incorporate relevant outside information.

- Support the theme with relevant facts, examples, and details.

- Use a logical and clear plan of organization.

- Introduce the theme by establishing a framework that is beyond a simple statement of the **Task** or **Historical Context**.

- Conclude the essay with a summation of the theme.

Activity 2

Part I: Multiple-Choice Questions

Expanding Zones of Exchange and Encounter

DIRECTIONS Read each question and circle the number of the best response.

Base your answer to question 1 on the diagram below and on your knowledge of social studies.

Early Indian Empires

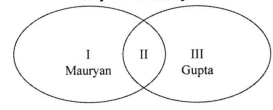

1   What information best fits in the area labeled "III"?

   (1) Small kingdoms consolidate.
   (2) Aryans migrate into Northern India.
   (3) Ashoka converts to Buddhism.
   (4) Hinduism becomes India's main religion.

2   Which is a result of the Crusades?

   (1) expulsion of the Moors from Europe
   (2) weakening of monarchies in Europe
   (3) increased trade between Europe and Asia
   (4) improved relations between Muslims, Jews, and Christians

3   Constantinople's location made it

   (1) the agricultural heartland of Europe
   (2) isolated from Asia's major trade routes
   (3) a city with architecture inspired by several civilizations
   (4) a holy city for Hindus and Buddhists

4   Cyril and Methodius helped Christianity spread to Russia by

   (1) marrying Justinian's sisters
   (2) creating an alphabet for the Slavonic language
   (3) supporting Roman Catholicism
   (4) moving Russia's capital to Moscow

5   According to the Qur'an, women are

   (1) equal to men before Allah
   (2) the head of the family
   (3) always required to wear a veil
   (4) able to have many husbands

6   Which of the following spread from India to Europe with the help of Arab traders?

(1) number system
(2) gunpowder
(3) printing press
(4) feudalism

Base your answer to question 7 on the graphic below and on your knowledge of social studies.

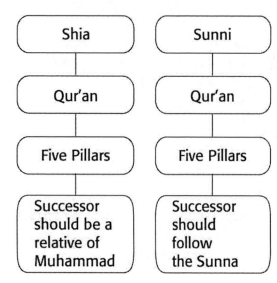

7   What was the main cause of division between Shia and Sunni Muslims?

(1) basic religious beliefs
(2) location of the Muslim capital
(3) succession of leadership
(4) division of landownership

8   Which aspect of Japanese civilization was **least** influenced by contact with other civilizations?

(1) Shinto
(2) pagoda architecture
(3) written language
(4) Buddhism

9   The Byzantine Empire and Russia were connected by trade and their

(1) common leadership under Alexander Nevsky
(2) support for the spread of Islam
(3) rejection of Christianity as it developed in Western Europe
(4) alliance with the Mongols

10   Which development stimulated cultural diffusion between the Mediterranean region and sub-Saharan Africa?

(1) opening of the Silk Road
(2) travels of Marco Polo
(3) Mongol invasions
(4) spread of Islam

11 Gunpowder, the compass, and movable type are technological innovations that occured during the

(1) Shang and Han dynasties in China
(2) Song and Tang dynasties in China
(3) Mauryan and Gupta empires in India
(4) Harappan and Vedic periods in India

12 During the Song dynasty, neo-Confucianism

(1) stopped the Mongols from invading
(2) reduced cultural ties with Korea
(3) ended the Period of Disunion
(4) helped reform the civil service examination system

13 Who established the Frankish Empire?

(1) Charlemagne
(2) Saladin
(3) Richard the Lion-hearted
(4) Pope Urban II

14 Which is *least* associated with feudalism in Europe?

(1) lords
(2) vassals
(3) serfs
(4) monks

15 The combination of Christian faith with rational thought during the Middle Ages became known as

(1) alchemy
(2) chivalry
(3) feudalism
(4) scholasticism

16 The Justinian Code

(1) was the main inspiration for the Shari'ah
(2) systematized the laws of the Byzantine Empire
(3) was the main cause of the rise of monarchies in Europe
(4) obligated vassals to defend their king

17 The manorial system primarily concerned which of the following?

(1) relations with the church
(2) economic activity
(3) vassal disputes
(4) town government

Activity 2

Part I: Multiple-Choice Questions

Expanding Zones of Exchange and Encounter

18 How were Chinese influences introduced to Japan during the mid-500s?

(1) on the Silk Roads
(2) across a land bridge
(3) by sea
(4) across the Sahara

Base your answer to question 19 on the passage below and on your knowledge of social studies.

"All south from this is named the Middle Kingdom . . . The people are numerous and happy . . . Throughout the whole country the people do not kill any living creature . . . The only exception is that of the Chandalas. That is the name for those who are (held to be) wicked men, and live apart from others. When they enter the gate of a city . . . they . . . make themselves known, so that men know and avoid them, and do not come into contact with them."

—Faxian

19 This excerpt *most* concerns an aspect of India's

(1) social structure
(2) religious traditions
(3) writing system
(4) trade network

20 During the Ottoman Empire, "People of the book" were allowed to

(1) translate writings into Arabic
(2) open schools to teach the Qur'an
(3) practice their religious beliefs
(4) found monasteries

Activity 2   Part II: Thematic Essay
_____
Expanding Zones of Exchange and Encounter

Answers to the essay questions are to be written on a separate sheet of paper.

In developing your answer to Part II, be sure to keep these general definitions in mind:

(a) *Describe* means "to tell about or illustrate something in words."

(b) *Discuss* means "to make observations about something by using facts, reasoning, and argument; to present in some detail."

PART II: THEMATIC ESSAY QUESTION
DIRECTIONS Write a well-organized essay that includes an introduction, several paragraphs addressing the task below, and a conclusion.

THEME Cultural and Intellectual Life

> Muslim civilization developed states that touched three continents and produced some of history's most notable achievements in the arts and sciences

TASK Discuss Muslim civilization and its contribution to global history.

> - Describe how Islamic texts inspired a culture of learning and achievement.
> - Discuss the connections between Muslim scholars and the scholars of ancient Greece.
> - Describe Muslim contributions to scholarship, the arts, and architecture.

You may use any example from your study of global history. Some suggestions that you might wish to consider include Muslim contributions to geography, astronomy, mathematics, medicine, literature, calligraphy, and architecture.

You are *not* limited to these suggestions.

GUIDELINES
In your essay, be sure to

- Develop all aspects of the task.
- Support the theme with relevant facts, examples, and details.
- Use a logical and clear plan of organization, including an introduction and a conclusion that are beyond a restatement of the theme.

Activity 2   Part III: Document-Based Activity
Expanding Zones of Exchange and Encounter

Part A: Using Source Materials

HISTORICAL CONTEXT As European and Islamic civilizations developed, so, too, did their curiosity about other civilizations. By the 1100s and 1200s contact between many of the world's civilizations was well established. Sparked by curiosity, warfare, and the desire for trade, travelers from various civilizations journeyed to parts of the world that were new to them. As they did so, these foreign travelers gained knowledge about the cultures, climates, and governments of other civilizations.

TASK Using information from the documents and your knowledge of world history, answer the questions that follow each document in Part A. Your answers to the questions will help you write the Part B essay.

DIRECTIONS Examine the following documents and answer the questions that follow each document.

DOCUMENT 1

> The land of Zanj [in East Africa] produces wild leopard skins. The people wear them as clothes, or export them to Muslim countries. They are the largest leopard skins and the most beautiful for making saddles . . . They also export tortoise-shell for making combs, for which ivory is likewise used . . . The Zanj are settled in that area, which stretches as far as Sofala [in Mozambique], which is the furthest limit of the land and the end of the voyages made from Oman and Siraf [in Iran] on the sea of Zanj . . . It is from this country that come tusks weighing fifty pounds and more. They usually go to Oman, and from there are sent to China and India. This is the chief trade route . . .
>
> —Arab historian and geographer Al-Masudi, 916

From "Land of Zanj" by Al-Masudi from *History of Africa* by Kevin Shillington. Published by St. Martin's Press, New York, 1995.

1. What trade goods came from the land of Zanj?

_____

2. With which other peoples did the people of Zanj trade?

_____

_____

Activity 2   Part III: Document-Based Activity

Expanding Zones of Exchange and Encounter

DOCUMENT 2

> These [Jewish] merchants . . . speak Persian, Roman [Greek and Latin], Arabic, and the Frankish, Spanish, and Slav languages. They travel from West to East and from East to West, sometimes by land, sometimes by sea. From the West they bring back eunuchs, female slaves, boys, silk, furs, and spices. They sail from the country of the Franks, on the Western Sea [Mediterranean Sea], and head towards Farama [in northern Egypt] . . . there they load their goods on the backs of beasts of burden and take the land route to Qulzum [Suez], a five days' journey, at a distance of 20 parasangs. They set sail on the Eastern Sea [the Red Sea] and make their way from Qulzum to Al Jar and Jidda; thence they go to Sind, India, and China. On their return they load up with musk, aloes, camphor, cinnamon, and other products of the Eastern countries, and come back to Qulzum, and then to Farama, where they again set sail on the Western Sea. Some head for Constantinople to sell their goods; others make their way to the country of the Franks.
>
> —Arab geographer Ibn Khurdadhbih, 847

From *History of the Indian Ocean* by Auguste Toussaint, translated by June Guicharnaud.
Copyright © 1966 by **University of Chicago Press**. Reproduced by permission of the publisher.

3. To what different places did Jewish merchants travel?

_____

_____

_____

4. What goods did the Jewish merchants exchange?

_____

_____

_____

Activity 2   Part III: Document-Based Activity

Expanding Zones of Exchange and Encounter

DOCUMENT 3

Before You Read The following words in the document below may be
new to you: *sumpter, supplication*. You may want to look them up in a
dictionary.

> The [Turkish] caravan, with all its riches, became the spoil of the victors
> [the Crusaders]. Its guards surrendered to our soldiers themselves, their
> beasts of burden, and sumpter horses; and stretching forth their hands in
> supplication, they implored for mercy, on condition only that their lives
> should be spared. They led the yoked horses and camels by the halter, and
> offered them to our men, and they brought mules loaded with spices of
> different kinds, and of great value; gold and silver; cloaks of silk; purple
> and scarlet robes, and variously-ornamented apparel, besides arms and
> weapons of divers[e] forms; coats of mail, commonly called *gasiganz*;
> costly cushions, pavilions, tents, biscuit, bread, barley, grain, meal, and a
> large quantity of conserves [a medicinal preparation] and medicines;
> basins, bladders, chess-boards; silver dishes and candlesticks; pepper,
> cinnamon, sugar, and wax; and other valuables of choice and various
> kinds; an immense sum of money, and an incalculable quantity of goods,
> such as had never before (as we have said) been taken at one and the same
> time, in any former battle.
>
> —Geoffrey de Vinsauf, *Itinerary of Richard I
> and Others, to the Holy Land*, 1192

5. Geoffrey de Vinsauf describes the taking of a Turkish trade caravan by the army of
England's Richard I during the Crusades. What goods did English soldiers seize from
the caravan?

_____

_____

_____

6. Why might disrupting trade caravans have been important to the English?

_____

_____

_____

Activity 2 | Part III: Document-Based Activity

Expanding Zones of Exchange and Encounter

DOCUMENT 4

Before You Read The following words in the document below may be
new to you: *profusion*, *embossed*. You may want to look them up in a
dictionary.

There is pepper here [in Gujarat, India] in profusion and also ginger and
indigo. There is also plenty of cotton, for the cotton trees grow here to a
great height—as much as six paces after twenty years' growth. But when
they reach this age they no longer produce cotton fit for spinning, but only
for use in wadding or padded quilts . . .

The manufactures of this kingdom include great quantities of leather
goods, that is, the tanned hides of goat and buffalo, wild ox and unicorn
and many other beasts. Enough is manufactured to load several ships a
year. They are exported to Arabia and many other countries . . . They also
manufacture handsome mats of scarlet leather, embossed with birds and
beasts and stitched with gold and silver of very fine workmanship . . . They
also make cushions stitched with gold, so splendid that they are worth fully
six marks of silver . . . some are of such a quality that they are worth ten
marks of silver.

—Marco Polo, *The Travels of Marco Polo*, c. 1295

From *The Travels of Marco Polo*, translated by Ronald Latham (Penguin Classics, 1958).
Copyright © 1958 by Ronald Latham. Reproduced by permission of **Penguin Books Ltd**.

7. What Indian trade goods does Marco Polo describe?

_____

_____

_____

8. What effect might Marco Polo's report have had on European merchants?

_____

_____

_____

DOCUMENT 5

Before You Read The following words in the document below may be
new to you: *vessel*, *disembarking*. You may want to look them up in a
dictionary.

> On leaving Zayla we sailed for fifteen days and came to Maqdasha
> [Mogadishu], which is an enormous town. Its inhabitants are merchants
> and have many camels, of which they slaughter hundreds every day [for
> food]. When a vessel reaches the port, it is met by sumbuqs, which are
> small boats, in each of which are a number of young men, each carrying a
> covered dish containing food. He presents this to one of the merchants on
> the ship saying "This is my guest," and all the others do the same. Each
> merchant on disembarking goes only to the house of the young man who is
> his host, except those who have made frequent journeys to the town and
> know its people well; these live where they please. The host then sells his
> goods for him and buys for him, and if anyone buys anything from him at
> too low a price, or sells to him in the absence of his host, the sale is
> regarded by them as invalid. This practice is of great advantage to them.
>
> —Muslim traveler Ibn Battuta, *Travels in Asia and Africa*, c. 1325–1354

From *Travels in Asia and Africa 1325–1354* by Ibn Battuta, translated by H.A.R. Gibb.
Copyright 1929 by Broadway House, London. Reproduced by permission of **David Higham
Associates Limited**.

9. How did Muslim merchants obtain goods from traders in Maqdasha?

_____

_____

_____

10. Why might Maqdasha have been a popular place to trade?

_____

_____

_____

_____

Activity 2 | Part III: Document-Based Activity
Expanding Zones of Exchange and Encounter

DOCUMENT 6

Before You Read The following words in the document below may be new to you: *revenue, victuals*. You may want to look them up in a dictionary.

> **Chapter 2.** From that country I passed to Tauris [Tabriz in Iran], a great city and a royal, which anciently was called Susis, and was the city of the King Ahasuerus. In it they say the Arbor Secco existeth in a mosque, that is to say, in a church of the Saracens [Muslims]. And this is a nobler city and a better for merchandise than any other which at this day existeth in the world. For there is not on the face of the earth any kind of provision, or any species of goods, but you will find great store thereof at Tauris. It is admirable for situation, and so opulent a city that you would scarcely believe the things to be found there; for the whole world, almost, hath dealings with that city for merchandise. And the Christians will tell you that the emperor there hath more revenue from that one city than the king of France hath from his whole realm . . .
>
> **Chapter 21.** In the neighborhood of that realm is a great island, Java by name, which hath a compass of a good three thousand miles. And the king of it hath subject to himself seven crowned kings. Now this island is populous exceedingly, and is the second best of all islands that exist. For in it grow camphor, cubebs, cardamoms, nutmegs, and many other precious spices. It hath also very great store of all victuals save wine.
>
> —Friar Odoric of Friuli, *Relatio: The Eastern Parts of the World Described*, c. 1330

11. What trade goods does Friar Odoric see on his travels to Iran and Java?

_____

_____

_____

12. Why might Friar Odoric's report of his journey have proved valuable to the people of Europe?

_____

_____

_____

Activity 2   Part III: Document-Based Activity

Expanding Zones of Exchange and Encounter

DOCUMENT 7

On 9 August the [Portuguese] ships left Kilwa for Mombasa, sixty leagues up the coast. The ship Sam Rafael reached there on 14 August, but the Grand-Captain arrived with the other ten ships a day earlier . . .

Mombasa is a very large town and lies on an island from one and a half to two leagues round. The town is built on rocks on the higher part of the island and has no walls on the side of the sea; but on the land side it is protected by a wall as high as the fortress . . .

The Grand-Captain ordered that the town should be sacked and that each man should carry off to his ship whatever he found: so that at the end there would be a division of the spoil, each man to receive a twentieth of what he found. The same rule was made for gold, silver, and pearls. Then everyone started to plunder the town and to search the houses, forcing open the doors with axes and iron bars. There was a large quantity of cotton cloth for Sofala in the town, for the whole coast gets its cotton cloth from here. So the Grand-Captain got a good share of the trade of Sofala for himself. A large quantity of rich silk and gold embroidered clothes was seized, and carpets also; one of these, which was without equal for beauty, was sent to the King of Portugal together with many other valuables.

—Hans Mayr, *The Voyage and Acts of Dom Francisco*, c. 1505

---

13. How did the Portuguese obtain trade goods from the people of Mombasa?

_____

_____

_____

14. What trade goods did the Portuguese obtain?

_____

_____

_____

Activity 2

Part III: Document-Based Activity

Expanding Zones of Exchange and Encounter

Part B: Writing a Document-Based Essay

HISTORICAL CONTEXT As European and Islamic civilizations developed, so, too, did their curiosity about other civilizations. By the 1100s and 1200s contact between many of the world's civilizations was well established. Sparked by curiosity, warfare, and the desire for trade, travelers from various civilizations journeyed to parts of the world that were new to them. As they did so, these foreign travelers gained knowledge about the cultures, climates, and governments of other civilizations.

TASK Using information from the documents and your knowledge of world history, write an essay in which you:

- Discuss the contact that took place between various civilizations between AD 800 and 1400 and the attitudes that travelers had toward the areas and people they encountered on their journeys.

DIRECTIONS Using the information from the documents provided and your knowledge of world history, write a well-organized essay that includes an introduction, a body of several paragraphs, and a conclusion. In the body of the essay, use examples from at least *five* documents. Support your response with relevant facts, examples, and details. Include additional outside information.

GUIDELINES
In your essay, be sure to:

- Address all aspects of the **Task** by accurately analyzing and interpreting at least *five* documents.
- Incorporate information from the documents in the body of the essay.
- Incorporate relevant outside information.
- Support the theme with relevant facts, examples, and details.
- Use a logical and clear plan of organization.
- Introduce the theme by establishing a framework that is beyond a simple statement of the **Task** or **Historical Context**.
- Conclude the essay with a summation of the theme.

DIRECTIONS Read each question and circle the number of the best response.

Base your answer to question 1 on the map below and on your knowledge of social studies.

Ghana (800s–1070s)	Gold–salt trade
Mali (1230s–1430s)	Gold–salt trade; Muslim
Songhai (1460s–1591)	Trans-Saharan trade; Muslim

1   Which of the following titles best completes the table?

(1) Cities of Great Zimbabwe
(2) East African Kingdoms
(3) Ethiopia's Muslim States
(4) West African Trading Empires

2   Whose book about life among Japan's ruling class is considered one of the world's first novels?

(1) Confucius
(2) Kublai Khan
(3) Lady Murasaki Shikibu
(4) Marco Polo

3   Which East African civilization developed unique religious traditions because of trade connections?

(1) Mali
(2) Ghana
(3) Songhai
(4) Axum

4   In the mid-1400s, Johannes Gutenberg was responsible for

(1) religious reform
(2) mapmaking improvements
(3) innovations in printing
(4) expansion of the spice trade

5   Portugal contributed to the resurgence of Europe during the Renaissance by

(1) increasing long-distance trade
(2) reforming the Roman Catholic Church
(3) establishing the first absolute monarchy
(4) abolishing medieval guilds

6   Which person's ideas most contributed to the renewed emphasis on secularism associated with the Italian Renaissance?

(1) Gerardus Mercator
(2) Nicholas Copernicus
(3) Martin Luther
(4) Desiderius Erasmus

Activity 3

Part I: Multiple-Choice Questions

Global Interactions

7 William Shakespeare was responsible for innovations in

(1) politics
(2) literature
(3) painting
(4) science

Base your answer to question 8 on the chart below and on your knowledge of social studies.

Fuedal Obligations	
Fuedal Lord	• Give land • Protect from attack • Resolve disputes between knights
Vassal	• Provide military service • Remain loyal and faithful • Give money on special occasions

8 Which of the following bound lords and knights together in a system of mutual service in the Middle Ages?

(1) fealty oaths
(2) the selling of fiefs
(3) the manor economy
(4) religious piety

9 What was the city of Timbuktu's historical significance?

(1) It was the capital of the Mongolian Empire.
(2) It was the birthplace of the Northern Renaissance.
(3) It was an important trade center in Songhai.
(4) It was where the Black Death started.

10 Which statement is true about the Mongols' rule of China?

(1) It brought about the end of the Yuan dynasty.
(2) It benefited China's economy because trade expanded.
(3) It resulted in Islam's becoming China's main religion.
(4) It resulted in Japan's becoming a Chinese colony.

11 One factor that caused the rise of humanism in southern Europe was

(1) increased contact with Muslims who had preserved Greek and Roman writings
(2) religious change associated with the Protestant Reformation
(3) religious change associated with the Catholic Counter-Reformation
(4) exposure to Chinese philosophies

12 The start of the Renaissance is most associated with rapid economic growth in which city?

(1) Paris
(2) Venice
(3) Moscow
(4) Constantinople

13 Historians think that the **most** likely way the Black Death spread to Europe was the movement of

(1) knights between Europe and the Holy Land during the Crusades
(2) merchants along trade routes passing through Central Asia
(3) sailors and slaves between Africa, and the Americas
(4) refugees during the Wars of the Roses

14 Ibn Battuta and Marco Polo contributed to global interaction by

(1) founding the Hanseatic League.
(2) writing about their travels.
(3) exploring the Americas.
(4) inventing navigational devices.

15 Who was **least** associated with the religious controversy between Roman Catholics and Protestants?

(1) Niccolò Machiavelli
(2) John Calvin
(3) Henry VIII
(4) Martin Luther

16 The leader who helped create an empire that spanned from China to the edge of Europe was

(1) Genghis Khan
(2) Saladin
(3) Richard the Lion-hearted
(4) Mansa Musa

17 The rise of Ghana can be attributed to that kingdom's large supply of

(1) gold and location near the edge of the Sahara
(2) slaves and location on the shores of the Indian Ocean
(3) sugar and location in the Caribbean Basin
(4) gunpowder and location at the Strait of Malacca

18 The Pax Mongolica was the

(1) trade route between the Mongol Empire and India
(2) period of peace and stability created by the Mongol Empire
(3) Chinese alphabet adapted for Mongol use
(4) title given to the Mongol leader Kublai Khan by the Chinese

Base your answer to question 19 on the passage below and on your knowledge of social studies.

> "There was no person, officer of the court, or holder of any office of the sultanate who did not receive a sum of gold from [Mansa Musa] . . . So much gold was current in Cairo [Egypt] that it ruined the value of money."
>
> —*Ibn Fadl Allah al-Omari*
> *c. 1300s*

19 The excerpt concerns

  (1) a Malian king's religious pilgrimage to Mecca
  (2) a European trader's travels along the Silk Road
  (3) how the Italian city-states came to dominate trade with Asia
  (4) why the Chinese discontinued overseas exploration

20 The two historical developments *most* directly related to each other were the rise of

  (1) humanism and the Black Death
  (2) nationalism and absolute monarchies
  (3) Venice and the Mongol Empire
  (4) Japanese and European feudalism

Activity 3

Part II: Thematic Essay

Global Interactions

Answers to the essay questions are to be written on a separate sheet of paper.

In developing your answer to Part II, be sure to keep these general definitions in mind:

(a) *Discuss* means "to make observations about something by using facts, reasoning, and argument; to present in some detail."

(b) *Explain* means "to make plain or understandable; to give reasons for or causes of; to show the logical development or relationships of."

(c) *Describe* means "to tell about or to illustrate something in words."

PART II: THEMATIC ESSAY QUESTION

DIRECTIONS Write a well-organized essay that includes an introduction, several paragraphs addressing the task below, and a conclusion.

THEME **Conflict**

> Throughout history, conflicts between groups of people have resulted in important historical change.

TASK Identify *two* conflicts, one from the Protestant Reformation and one from the Counter-Reformation, that led to religious reform in Europe during 1500s and for *each*

> - Discuss the major reasons for the conflict.
> - Explain the sequence of events leading up to the conflict.
> - Describe the lasting changes the conflict had on religion.

You may choose any example from your study of the Protestant Reformation and the Counter-Reformation. Some suggestions that you might wish to consider include dissatisfaction with the Catholic Church, the role of religious reformers, such as Martin Luther and John Calvin, in the Protestant Reformation, Henry VIII's breaking from the Catholic Church, and the Inquisition.

You are *not* limited to these suggestions.

GUIDELINES

In your essay, be sure to

- Develop all aspects of the task.
- Support the theme with relevant facts, examples, and details.
- Use a logical and clear plan of organization, including an introduction and a conclusion that are beyond a restatement of the theme.

Activity 3

Part III: Document-Based Activity

Global Interactions

Part A: Using Source Materials

HISTORICAL CONTEXT In the 1300s and 1400s the Renaissance brought a revival in learning to Europe. New ideas about art, literature, education, and politics began to take hold. In the 1500s these ideas influenced the Protestant Reformation and the Scientific Revolution, and new attitudes toward religion and science soon spread throughout Europe. As these new ideas spread, Europe left the Middle Ages behind and entered a new period in history, sometimes called the Modern Age.

TASK Using information from the documents and your knowledge of world history, answer the questions that follow each document in Part A. Your answers to the questions will help you write the Part B essay.

DIRECTIONS Examine the following documents and answer the questions that follow each document.

DOCUMENT 1

> Luther . . . explained in many of his writings to what extent, and on what grounds, a change must needs be effected in human rites and traditions; what form of doctrine he wished to retain, and what administration of the sacraments he most approved . . . and are apparent both from the rites of the church in that city, and from the doctrine with which our church [the Lutheran Church] now resounds . . .
>
> I relate these circumstances, not only for the information of pious men as to the errors which Luther attacked and the idols which he removed, but to convince them that he embraced every important doctrine of the Church, restored purity to its ritual, and exhibited models of reform such as is desirable in Christian churches; and it is well that posterity should be made acquainted with the views held by Luther.
>
> —Philip Melancthon, *A History of the Life and Actions of the Very Reverend Dr. Martin Luther*, 1549

1. How did Martin Luther bring change to religion in the 1500s, and what was the impact of those changes?

_____

_____

_____

DOCUMENT 2

Before You Read The following words in the document below may be
new to you: *annihilates, intuition, certitude, combustible.* You may want to
look them up in a dictionary.

> Having laid down the main points of the wisdom of the Latins as regards
> language, mathematics and optics, I wish now to review the principles of
> wisdom from the point of view of experimental science, because without
> experiment it is impossible to know anything thoroughly.
>
> There are two ways of acquiring knowledge, one through reason, the
> other by experiment. Argument reaches a conclusion and compels us to
> admit it, but it neither makes us certain nor so annihilates doubt that the
> mind rests calm in the intuition of truth, unless it finds this certitude by
> way of experience. Thus many have arguments toward attainable facts, but
> because they have not experienced them, they overlook them and neither
> avoid a harmful nor follow a beneficial course. Even if a man that has
> never seen fire, proves by good reasoning that fire burns, and devours and
> destroys things, nevertheless the mind of one hearing his arguments would
> never be convinced, nor would he avoid fire until he puts his hand or some
> combustible thing into it in order to prove by experiment what the
> argument taught. But after the fact of combustion is experienced, the mind
> is satisfied and lies calm in the certainty of truth. Hence argument is not
> enough, but experience is.
>
> —Roger Bacon, *On Experimental Science,*
>
> 1268

2. What new idea or method does Bacon promote? Why does he think it is important?

_____

_____

_____

3. In what ways has this new idea or method been important?

_____

_____

_____

Activity 3   Part III: Document-Based Activity

Global Interactions

DOCUMENT 3

Before You Read The following words in the document below may be
new to you: *obstinacy, diligence, counterfeited.* You may want to look
them up in a dictionary.

> He [Leonardo da Vinci] also painted in Milan, for the Friars of S. Dominic,
> at S. Maria dell Grazie, a Last Supper, a most beautiful and marvellous
> thing; and to the heads of the Apostles he gave such majesty and beauty,
> that he left the head of Christ unfinished, not believing that he was able to
> give it that divine air which is essential to the image of Christ. This work,
> remaining thus all but finished, has ever been held by the Milanese in the
> greatest veneration, and also by strangers as well; for Leonardo imagined
> and succeeded in expressing that anxiety which had seized the Apostles in
> wishing to know who should betray their Master. For which reason in all
> their faces are seen love, fear, and wrath, or rather, sorrow, at not being
> able to understand the meaning of Christ; which thing excites no less
> marvel than the sight, in contrast to it, of obstinacy, hatred, and treachery
> in Judas; not to mention that every least part of the work displays an
> incredible diligence, seeing that even in the tablecloth the texture of the
> stuff is counterfeited in such a manner that linen itself could not seem more
> real.
>
> —Giorgio Vasari, *Lives of the Most Eminent Italian Architects,*
> *Painters, and Sculptors*, 1550

4. According to Vasari, what were some of Leonardo da Vinci's accomplishments as a
painter?

_____

_____

_____

5. How might these accomplishments have influenced later art in Europe?

_____

_____

_____

DOCUMENT 4

Before You Read The following words in the document below may be new to you: *pre-eminences, jurisdictions, commodities, redress.* You may want to look them up in a dictionary.

> Be it enacted by authority of this present Parliament that the king our sovereign lord, his heirs and successors kings of the realm shall be taken, accepted and reputed the only supreme head on earth of the Church of England called Anglicana Ecclesia, and shall have and enjoy annexed and united to the imperial crown of this realm as well the title and style thereof, as all honours, dignities, pre-eminences, jurisdictions, privileges, authorities, immunities, profits and commodities to the said dignity of supreme head of the same Church belonging and appertaining. And that from time to time to visit, repress, redress, reform, order, correct, restrain, and amend all such errors, heresies, abuses, offences, contempts, and enormities whatsoever they be, which by any manner [of] spiritual authority or jurisdiction ought or may lawfully be reformed, repressed redressed, ordered, corrected, restrained, or amended, most to the pleasure of Almighty God the increase of virtue in Christ's religion and for the conservation of the peace, unity, and tranquillity of this realm.
>
> —The Act of Supremacy, 1534

6. What did the Act of Supremacy change in England?

_____

_____

_____

7. What might have been the results of such a change?

_____

_____

_____

Activity 3

Part III: Document-Based Activity

Global Interactions

DOCUMENT 5
Gutenberg inspects a page that has just been printed
c. 1600s

© Bettmann/CORBIS

8. What new form of technology is illustrated in this image?

_____

_____

_____

9. What were the effects of this innovation?

_____

_____

_____

DOCUMENT 6

Before You Read The following words in the document below may be
new to you: *cosmology, exposition, planetary, earnestness.* You may want
to look them up in a dictionary.

> I had learned that you had not merely mastered the discoveries of the
> ancient astronomers uncommonly well but had also formulated a new
> cosmology. In it you maintain that the earth moves; that the sun occupies
> the lowest, and thus the central, place in the universe; that the eighth
> heaven remains perpetually motionless and fixed; and that, together with
> the elements included in its sphere, the moon, situated between the heavens
> of Mars and Venus, revolves around the sun in the period of a year. I have
> also learned that you have written an exposition of this whole system of
> astronomy, and have computed the planetary motions and set them down in
> tables, to the greatest admiration of all. Therefore with the utmost
> earnestness I entreat you, most learned sir, unless I inconvenience you, to
> communicate this discovery of yours to scholars.
>
> —Nicholas Schönberg, the cardinal of Capua,
> letter to Nicolaus Copernicus, 1536

From "Letter of Nicholas Schönberg, Rome, 1 November 1536" from *On the Revolutions* by
Nicholas Copernicus, edited by Jerzy Dobrzycki and translated with commentary by Edward
Rosen. Copyright © 1978 by Edward Rosen. Reproduced by permission of **Johns Hopkins
University Press.**

10. According to this letter, what discoveries has Copernicus made?

_____

_____

11. What effect might Copernicus's discoveries have had on science and society?

_____

_____

_____

Activity 3

Part III: Document-Based Activity

Global Interactions

DOCUMENT 7

Before You Read The following words in the document below may be
new to you: *spyglass, credence, refraction*. You may want to look them up
in a dictionary.

> About 10 months ago a report reached my ears that a certain Fleming had
> constructed a spyglass by means of which visible objects, though very
> distant from the eye of the observer, were distinctly seen as if nearby. Of
> this truly remarkable effect several experiences were related, to which
> some persons gave credence while others denied them. A few days later the
> report was confirmed to me in a letter from a noble Frenchman at Paris,
> Jacques Badovere, which caused me to apply myself wholeheartedly to
> investigate means by which I might arrive at the invention of a similar
> instrument. This I did soon afterwards, my basis being the doctrine of
> refraction.
>
> —Galileo Galilei, *Starry Messenger*, 1610

From *Starry Messenger* by Galileo Galilei from *Telescope, Tides, and Tactics* by Stillman
Drake. Copyright © 1983 by Stillman Drake. Reproduced by permission of **University of
Chicago Press**.

12. To what device is Galileo referring?

_____

_____

_____

13. How has this device influenced learning since its invention?

_____

_____

_____

Part B: Writing a Document-Based Essay

HISTORICAL CONTEXT In the 1300s and 1400s the Renaissance brought a revival in learning to Europe. New ideas about art, literature, education, and politics began to take hold. In the 1500s these ideas influenced the Protestant Reformation and Scientific Revolution, and new attitudes toward religion and science soon spread throughout Europe. As these new ideas spread, Europe left the Middle Ages behind and entered a new period in history, sometimes called the Modern Age.

TASK Using information from the documents and your knowledge of world history, write an essay in which you:

- Discuss new artistic, religious, and scientific ideas and methods that were introduced in Europe from the 1300s to the 1600s.

- Identify the effects that these new ideas and methods have had on intellectual life in Europe and around the world.

DIRECTIONS Using the information from the documents provided and your knowledge of world history, write a well-organized essay that includes an introduction, a body of several paragraphs, and a conclusion. In the body of the essay, use examples from at least *five* documents. Support your response with relevant facts, examples, and details. Include additional outside information.

GUIDELINES
In your essay, be sure to:

- Address all aspects of the **Task** by accurately analyzing and interpreting at least *five* documents.

- Incorporate information from the documents in the body of the essay.

- Incorporate relevant outside information.

- Support the theme with relevant facts, examples, and details.

- Use a logical and clear plan of organization.

- Introduce the theme by establishing a framework that is beyond a simple statement of the **Task** or **Historical Context**.

- Conclude the essay with a summation of the theme.

Name _____ Class _____ Date _____

Activity 4

Part I: Multiple-Choice Questions

The First Global Age

DIRECTIONS Read each question and circle the number of the best response.

Base your answer to question 1 on the map below and on your knowledge of social studies.

Aztec Triple Alliance, 1431–1521

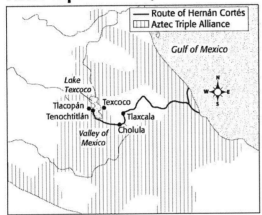

1   At the time of first contact with Europeans, the region of Mesoamerica under Aztec control supported

   (1) a heavily populated urban civilization
   (2) a sparsely populated rural society
   (3) three nation-states
   (4) hunter-gatherer groups only

2   The *encomienda* system was the

   (1) economic system Spain used in its Latin American colonies
   (2) movement against colonial rule in Spain
   (3) tribute that Triple Alliance members paid to Moctezuma
   (4) name Moctezuma gave to Hernán Cortés

3   In 1770 the dominant colonial power along the Atlantic coast of North America was

   (1) Spain
   (2) France
   (3) England
   (4) Portugal

4   The first major European voyages of exploration were sponsored by Prince Henry the Navigator of

   (1) Spain
   (2) England
   (3) Italy
   (4) Portugal

5   Which was a **main** factor in the establishment of the triangular trade route between Europe, Africa, and the Americas?

   (1) a land shortage in the Americas
   (2) a need for a large number of workers for plantations in the Americas
   (3) European demand for spices from India
   (4) reopening of the Silk Roads by the Ottoman Empire

Base your answer to question 6 on the map below and on your knowledge of social studies.

6   Which dynasty is known for producing this type of porcelain?

(1) the Ming
(2) the Ottoman
(3) the Qing
(4) the Mughal

7   What is Ferdinand Magellan best known for?

(1) leading the expedition that first circumnavigated the globe
(2) writing Magna Carta
(3) creating the *encomienda* system
(4) arguing that monarchs rule because of a "divine right"

8   In the 1400s Zheng He

(1) led the effort to overthrow Mongol rule in China
(2) led a series of Chinese naval expeditions
(3) restricted China's trade with Europe
(4) formed an alliance between China and the Aztec Empire

9   Hinduism, Buddhism, and Islam spread in Southeast Asia through

(1) Mongol conquests
(2) trade and missionaries
(3) the work of Marco Polo
(4) forced conversions

10 The end of Mongol rule led China's new dynasty to move toward cultural isolation and

(1) theocracy
(2) independent city-states
(3) parliamentary democracy
(4) absolutism

11 Which world region was part of the Ottoman Empire?

(1) Mesoamerica
(2) North Africa
(3) South America
(4) India

Activity 4   Part I: Multiple-Choice Questions

12 One similarity between the reign of the Ming dynasty in China and the reign of Ferdinand and Isabella in Spain was that they both

(1) supported Enlightenment ideas
(2) were involved in the armed expulsion of a foreign empire
(3) explored the Americas
(4) were signers of Magna Carta

Base your answer to question 13 on the passage below and on your knowledge of social studies.

"6. The common people will not be allowed to wear cotton clothing, under pain of death, but only garments of maguey [century plant] fiber . . .

7. No one but the great noblemen and chieftains is to build a house with a second story, under pain of death. No one is to put peaked or round gables upon his house. This privilege has been granted by the gods only to the great."

—From a law decreed by King Moctezuma I

13 This excerpt *best* illustrates which aspect of Aztec civilization?

(1) social structure
(2) clothing
(3) architecture
(4) economic system

14 The early kingdoms and empires of Southeast Asia were culturally *most* influenced by traders from

(1) Japan
(2) Russia
(3) China
(4) Ghana

15 Historians credit Suleyman I (the Great) with

(1) conquering Constantinople
(2) imposing one religion on the Ottoman Empire
(3) expanding the Ottoman Empire to its height of power in the 1500s
(4) introducing Islam to the Arabian Peninsula

16 The philosophy Thomas Hobbes described in *Two Treatises on Government* suggests that he would have supported the

(1) Puritan Revolution
(2) Scientific Revolution
(3) American Revolution
(4) French and Indian War

17 Which person contributed to the development of parliamentary democracy?

(1) Suleyman I
(2) Peter the Great
(3) Christopher Columbus
(4) John Locke

18 Which event *least* supports the statement that the period from 1450 to 1500 was a major turning point in global history?

(1) arrival of Europeans in the Americas
(2) fall of Constantinople to the Ottoman Empire
(3) launch of the Crusades
(4) expulsion of the Moors from Spain

19 Where did the Columbian Exchange result in a rapid decrease in population?

(1) Europe
(2) China
(3) North America
(4) Middle East

20 Which two colonial powers most influenced the development of Latin American culture?

(1) Netherlands and Spain
(2) Portugal and France
(3) Spain and Portugal
(4) France and England

Activity 4

Part II: Thematic Essay

The First Global Age

Answers to the essay questions are to be written on a separate sheet of paper.

In developing your answer to Part II, be sure to keep these general definitions in mind:

  (a) *Discuss* means "to make observations about something by using facts, reasoning, and argument; to present in some detail."

  (b) *Describe* means "to tell about or illustrate something in words."

  (c) *Evaluate* means to "examine and judge the significance, worth, or condition of; to determine the value of."

PART II: THEMATIC ESSAY QUESTION

DIRECTIONS Write a well-organized essay that includes an introduction, several paragraphs addressing the task below, and a conclusion.

THEME Human and Physical Geography

> The arrival of Christopher Columbus in the Americas in 1492 was a turning point in world history. In the years that followed Columbus's voyage, a biological and cultural exchange, called the Columbian Exchange, between Europeans and Native Americans changed societies worldwide.

TASK Discuss the Columbian Exchange and its lasting effects on societies worldwide.

> • Discuss how Native Americans and Europeans reacted to their encounters with one another.
>
> • Describe the exchange of plants, animals, and disease that occurred during the Columbian Exchange.
>
> • Evaluate *two* lasting effects of the Columbian Exchange on Native American societies and *two* of its effects on European societies.

You may choose any example from your study of global history. Some suggestions that you might wish to consider include changes in diet, health, population, and economic activities.

You are *not* limited to these suggestions.

GUIDELINES

In your essay, be sure to:

  • Develop all aspects of the task.

  • Support the theme with relevant facts, examples, and details.

  • Use a logical and clear plan of organization, including an introduction and a conclusion that are beyond a restatement of the theme.

Part III: Document-Based Activity

The First Global Age

Part A: Using Source Materials

HISTORICAL CONTEXT By the late 1400s Europeans had grown accustomed to having access to the riches and luxuries of China, India, and the islands of Southeast Asia. Traveling to and from these distant lands was difficult, and European explorers became determined to find sea routes to the East. Increasing European exploration led to many changes around the world.

TASK Using information from the documents and your knowledge of world history, answer the questions that follow each document in Part A. Your answers to the questions will help you write the Part B essay.

DIRECTIONS Examine the following documents and answer the questions that follow each document.

DOCUMENT 1

> Most High and Mighty Sovereigns, In obedience to your Highnesses' commands, and with submission to superior judgment, I will say whatever occurs to me in reference to the colonization and commerce of the Island of Espanola, and of the other islands, both those already discovered and those that may be discovered hereafter.
>
> In the first place, as regards the Island of Espanola: . . . the number of colonists who desire to go thither amounts to two thousand, owing to the land being safer and better for farming and trading, and . . . it will serve as a place to which they can return and from which they can carry on trade with the neighboring islands.
>
> —Christopher Columbus, letter to the king and queen of Spain, 1494

1. What was the island that was colonized?

_____

_____

2. How many people colonized the island, and why?

_____

_____

_____

Activity 4

Part III: Document-Based Activity

The First Global Age

DOCUMENT 2

> When the Portuguese began to import Asian spices by the sea route around Africa, this trade and the Spanish trade with America, were easily absorbed into the existing European pattern.
>
> Antwerp, in the Netherlands, became the richest trading city in Europe and the first great centre of world trade— in terms of the still very restricted volume of this trade, probably the greatest single centre of world trade in history. Its transoceanic trade was channelled through Spain and Portugal, and in the mid-sixteenth century the value of this trade amounted to about a fifth of Antwerp's total trade. England, Italy and the Baltic accounted for roughly an equal part and the remaining fifth was fairly evenly divided between trade with France and trade with Germany.
>
> —H. G. Koenigsberger, *Early Modern Europe 1500–1789*

From "Expansion and Reformation 1500–1600" from *Early Modern Europe 1500–1789* by H. G. Koenigsberger. Copyright © 1987 by H. G. Koenigsberger. Reproduced by permission of **Longman Inc.**

3. What did the Portuguese import by the sea route?

_____

_____

_____

4. What city became the richest trading city in Europe?

_____

_____

_____

DOCUMENT 3

Then [Montezuma] stood up to welcome Cortés; he came forward, bowed his head low and addressed him in these words: "Our lord, you are weary. The journey has tired you, but now you have arrived on the earth. You have come to your city, Mexico. You have come here to sit on your throne, to sit under its canopy . . .

"This was foretold by the kings who governed your city, and now it has taken place. You have come back to us; you have come down from the sky. Rest now, and take possession of your royal houses. Welcome to your land, my lords!"

When Motecuhzoma [Montezuma] had finished, La Malinche translated his address into Spanish so that the Captain could understand it. Cortés replied in his strange and savage tongue, speaking first to La Malinche: "Tell Motecuhzoma that we are his friends. There is nothing to fear. We have wanted to see him for a long time, and now we have seen his face and heard his words. Tell him that we love him well and that our hearts are contented." . . .

When this had been done, the celebrants began to sing their songs. That is how they celebrated the first day of the fiesta. On the second day they began to sing again, but without warning they were all put to death . . .

The Spaniards attacked the musicians first, slashing at their hands and faces until they had killed all of them . . . This slaughter in the Sacred Patio went on for three hours.

—An Aztec account of the conquest of Mexico, c. 1519

From *The Broken Spears: The Aztec Account of the Conquest of Mexico*, edited by Miguel Leon Portilla. Copyright © 1962 by Miguel Leon Portilla. Reproduced by permission of **Beacon Press, Boston, MA.**

5. How did Montezuma receive the Spanish?

_____

_____

6. What factor helped the Spanish conquer the powerful Aztec Empire?

_____

_____

_____

Activity 4

Part III: Document-Based Activity

The First Global Age

DOCUMENT 4

Before You Read The following words in the document below may be
new to you: *loathsome, pestilential, scarcely*. You may want to look them
up in a dictionary.

> The stench of the hold [where the slaves were kept below deck] while we
> were on the coast was so intolerably loathsome, that it was dangerous to
> remain there for any time, and some of us had been permitted to stay on the
> deck for fresh air; but now that the whole ship's cargo were confined
> together, it became absolutely pestilential. The closeness of the place, and
> the heat of the climate, added to the number in the ship which was so
> crowded that each had scarcely room to turn himself, almost suffocated us
> . . . This wretched situation was again aggravated by the galling of the
> chains, now become insupportable; and the filth of the necessary tubs, into
> which the children often fell, and were almost suffocated. The shrieks of
> the women, and the groans of the dying, rendered the whole scene of
> horror almost inconceivable."
>
> —Olaudah Equiano, a former slave, *The Interesting Narrative of the Life of
> Olaudah Equiano, or Gustavus Vassa, the African*, 1789

7. What does Olaudah Equiano describe in this account?

_____

_____

_____

8. What were some of the conditions that slaves endured?

_____

_____

_____

DOCUMENT 5
Aztec illustration of natives suffering from an unknown illness

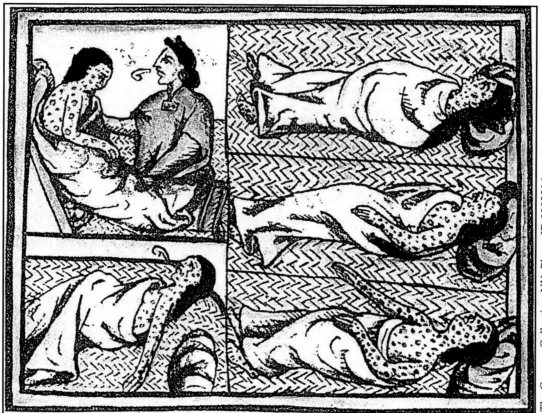

The Granger Collection, NY Photo ID 0002216

9. Look closely at this image. What does it show?

_____

_____

_____

10. How does this image illustrate the Columbian Exchange?

_____

_____

_____

Activity 4 | Part III: Document-Based Activity

The First Global Age

DOCUMENT 6

Sir, Believing that you will take pleasure in hearing of the great success which our Lord has granted me in my voyage, I write you this letter, whereby you will learn how in thirty-seven days' time I reached the Indies with the fleet which the most illustrious King and Queen, our sovereigns, gave to me, where I found very many islands thickly peopled, of all which I took possession without resistance for their Highnesses by proclamation made and with the royal standard unfurled . . . When I reached Juana [Cuba], I followed its coast to the westward, and found it so large that I thought it must be the mainland,—the province of Cathay [China]; and, as I found neither towns nor villages on the sea-coast, but only a few hamlets, with the inhabitants of which I could not hold a conversation because they all immediately fled, I kept on the same route, thinking that I could not fail to light upon some large cities and towns . . .

On my reaching the Indies, I took by force, in the first island that I discovered, some of these natives that they might learn our language and give me information in regard to what existed in these parts; and it so happened that they soon understood us and we them, either by words or signs, and they have been very serviceable to us. They are still with me, and from repeated conversations that I have had with them, I find that they still believe that I came from heaven.

—Christopher Columbus, letter to the secretary of the Spanish treasury,
February 1493

From "A letter to the secretary of the Spanish treasury, February 1493" by Christopher Columbus from *Renaissance and Reformation: 1300–1648*, edited by G. R. Elton. Copyright © 1976 by **Macmillan Publishing Company**. Reproduced by permission of the publisher.

11. Where did Columbus think he had landed when he reached Cuba?

_____

_____

_____

12. How did Columbus communicate with the people of the islands?

_____

_____

_____

DOCUMENT 7

Before You Read The following words in the document below may be
new to you: *commerce, innured* [also spelled *inured*], *procure*. You may
want to look them up in a dictionary.

> Kairouan, the largest town of the Maghrib, surpasses all others in its
> commerce, its riches, and the beauty of its buildings and bazaars. It is the
> seat of government of the whole Maghrib, the center to which flows the
> wealth of the land, and the residence of the sultan of that country. I heard
> from Abu al-Hasan head of the [public] treasury [in AD 947–48], that the
> income of all provinces and localities of the Maghrib . . . was between
> seven hundred and eight hundred million dinars . . .
>
> The exports from the Maghrib to the East are . . . European slaves,
> amber, silks, suits of very fine woolen, fineries, woolen skirts, carpets,
> iron, lead, mercury . . . People there possess excellent draft horses and
> camels innured to fatigue, which they procure from the Berbers.
>
> —A description of Muslim towns and trade in North Africa, c. 948

From "Descriptions of Towns" (retitled "Muslim towns and trade in North Africa") from *The
Medieval Town* by John H. Mundy and Peter Riesenberg. Copyright © 1958 and renewed
© 1986 by John H. Mundy and Peter Riesenberg. Reproduced by permission of **Wadsworth
Publishing Company.**

13. What were the chief exports of the Maghrib region?

_____

_____

_____

14. In what three areas did Kainouan surpass all the other towns?

_____

_____

_____

Activity 4 | Part III: Document-Based Activity

The First Global Age

Part B: Writing a Document-Based Essay

HISTORICAL CONTEXT By the late 1400s Europeans had grown accustomed to having access to the riches and luxuries of China, India, and the islands of Southeast Asia. Traveling to and from these distant lands was difficult, and European explorers became determined to find sea routes to the East. Increasing European exploration led to many changes around the world.

TASK Using information from the documents and your knowledge of world history, write an essay in which you:

- Discuss the positive and negative effects of European exploration.
- Identify the results of explorations in Europe and around the world.

DIRECTIONS Using the information from the documents provided and your knowledge of world history, write a well-organized essay that includes an introduction, a body of several paragraphs, and a conclusion. In the body of the essay, use examples from at least *five* documents. Support your response with relevant facts, examples, and details. Include additional outside information.

GUIDELINES
In your essay, be sure to:

- Address all aspects of the **Task** by accurately analyzing and interpreting at least *five* documents.
- Incorporate information from the documents in the body of the essay.
- Incorporate relevant outside information.
- Support the theme with relevant facts, examples, and details.
- Use a logical and clear plan of organization.
- Introduce the theme by establishing a framework that is beyond a simple statement of the **Task** or **Historical Context**.
- Conclude the essay with a summation of the theme.

DIRECTIONS Read each question and circle the number of the best response.

Base your answer to question 1 on the chart below and on your knowledge of social studies.

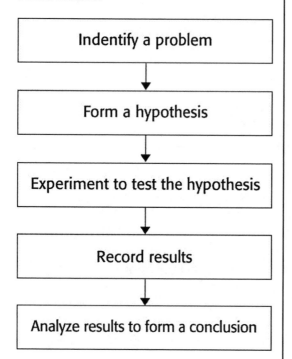

Indentify a problem

↓

Form a hypothesis

↓

Experiment to test the hypothesis

↓

Record results

↓

Analyze results to form a conclusion

1 The chart shows an approach to investigation called the
   (1) geocentric theory
   (2) heliocentric theory
   (3) scientific method
   (4) humanistic method

2 The primary purpose of the Congress of Vienna was to
   (1) restore the balance of power politics in Europe
   (2) negotiate peace terms between Europe and the Ottoman Empire
   (3) punish German military aggression
   (4) uphold political changes caused by the French Revolution

3 The power source that triggered a second wave of industrialization and improved the standard of living in cities in the late 1800s was
   (1) nuclear power
   (2) waterpower
   (3) electricity
   (4) steam

4 Which statement describes an idea associated with Karl Marx?
   (1) With great wealth comes great responsibility.
   (2) Workers should control farms and factories.
   (3) Food production cannot keep up with population growth.
   (4) Government regulation slows economic growth.

5   One social change that occurred during the Industrial Revolution was

(1) a decline in the size of the middle class

(2) the movement of middle class men and women into separate spheres

(3) mass migration to rural areas

(4) a decline in the standard of living over the long term

6   The Treaty of Nanjing is an example of an unequal treaty because it

(1) gave more privileges to some European nations than others

(2) required that British subjects be tried in Chinese courts

(3) gave Japan control over the Korean Peninsula

(4) benefited European nations at the expense of China

7   Who *most* contributed to the unification of Germany?

(1) Otto von Bismarck

(2) Napoleon Bonaparte

(3) Camillo di Cavour

(4) Klemens von Metternich

8   Which revolutionary general liberated most of northern South America from Spanish rule in the early 1800s?

(1) Toussaint L'Ouverture

(2) Simon Bolívar

(3) José de San Martín

(4) Porfirio Díaz

Base your answer to question 9 on the graphic below and on your knowledge of social studies.

English Textile Factories, Early 1800s

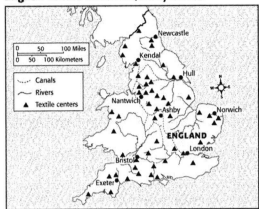

9   Which of the following would best explain why English textile factories were located near rivers and canals?

(1) River water powered waterwheels and provided transportation.

(2) Factories needed water for sanitation systems.

(3) Rivers connected factories with cotton plantations in rural England

(4) River water was used to irrigate cotton fields.

10 Conflict in the Balkan and Crimean regions and the rise of the nationalist group the Young Turks *most* concerned the

(1) British Empire
(2) Ottoman Empire
(3) "Scramble for Africa"
(4) Industrial Revolution

11 Unrest in Russia during the 1800s and early 1900s was a result of the czars' support of

(1) autocracy
(2) imperialism
(3) democracy
(4) socialism

12 One of the main reasons scholars during the Age of Enlightenment challenged traditional authorities was

(1) the Roman Catholic Church encouraged it
(2) exploration led to new discoveries that tradition did not address
(3) absolute monarchs believed challenging tradition would undermine parliamentary democracy
(4) there were new translations of classical Chinese philosophy

13 Which of the following was a cause of the French Revolution?

(1) economic prosperity
(2) strong leadership from king Louis XVI
(3) the influence of Enlightenment ideas
(4) new taxes on the ruling class

Base your answer to question 14 on the passage below and on your knowledge of social studies.

"The number of . . . machines . . . exceed all belief, being no less than *one hundred and seventy*! . . . . One machine will do as much work in one day as would otherwise employ twenty men. . . .Some say, Begin and learn some other business . . . How do we know we shall be any better for by the time we have served our second apprenticeship, another machine may arise, which may take away that business also."

— *Leeds Intelligencer* and *Leeds Mercury*, June 13, 1786

14 A person agreeing with the point of view expressed here would most likely support

(1) laissez-faire economics
(2) strong labor unions
(3) the French Revolution
(4) the Industrial Revolution

15 Which is the *best* example of the impact of nationalism in Europe?

(1) Adam Smith's economic ideas
(2) Karl Marx's economic ideas
(3) Industrial Revolution in Britain
(4) unification of Italy

Activity 5

Part I: Multiple-Choice Questions

An Age of Revolution

16 What was a cause of the Sepoy Mutiny?

(1) Britain closed Indian factories.

(2) The British army refused to recruit Indian soldiers.

(3) Indian soldiers believed that the British wanted them to abandon Islam and Hinduism.

(4) Sepoys were not allowed to trade with Britain.

17 The factor that *least* contributed to the development of imperialism was European

(1) demand for raw materials

(2) desire to adopt African and Asian cultural practices

(3) advantages in military technology

(4) interest in opening new markets

18 The growth in the number of people living in towns and cities is called

(1) civilization

(2) urbanization

(3) industrialization

(4) colonization

19 Public opinion regarding American independence decisively swung toward the Patriots after

(1) the Siege of Yorktown

(2) Thomas Paine wrote *Common Sense*

(3) the Boston Tea Party

(4) George Washington agreed to command the Continental Army

20 Adam Smith used reason to analyze

(1) government's role in economic growth

(2) social change caused by industrialization

(3) consequences of rapid population growth

(4) national independence movements

Activity 5

Part II: Thematic Essay

An Age of Revolution

Answers to the essay questions are to be written on a separate sheet of paper.

In developing your answer to Part II, be sure to keep these general definitions in mind:

    (a) *Discuss* means "to make observations about something using facts, reasoning, and argument; to present in some detail."

    (b) *Describe* means "to tell about or illustrate something in words."

    (c) *Explain* means "to make plain or understandable; to give reasons for or causes of; to show the logical development or relationships of."

PART II: THEMATIC ESSAY QUESTION

DIRECTIONS Write a well-organized essay that includes an introduction, several paragraphs addressing the task below, and a conclusion.

THEME Imperialism

> Imperialism is the process of one people ruling or controlling another. European imperialism was one of the most important causes of global historical change during the Age of Imperialism.

TASK Discuss the impact of imperialism in Europe and in one other world region.

> - Describe why European countries engaged in imperialism.
> - Discuss imperialism's effects on Europe.
> - Explain the effects of imperialism on another region or country.

You may choose any example from your study of global history. Some suggestions that you might wish to consider include European imperialism in Africa, China, Latin America, Japan, and India. You should limit your discussion of imperialism's impact to the period from 1750 to 1920.

You are *not* limited to these suggestions.

GUIDELINES

In your essay, be sure to

- Develop all aspects of the task.

- Support the theme with relevant facts, examples, and details.

- Use a logical and clear plan of organization, including an introduction and a conclusion that are beyond a restatement of the theme.

Activity 5   Part III: Document-Based Activity
_____
                                        An Age of Revolution

Part A: Using Source Materials

HISTORICAL CONTEXT In the 1800s a new spirit of nationalism swept across Europe and the Americas. In Europe, nationalism sparked revolutions and the formation of new nations. In Latin America, colonies won their independence from Europe.

TASK Using information from the documents and your knowledge of world history, answer the questions that follow each document in Part A. Your answers to the questions will help you write the Part B essay.

DIRECTIONS Examine the following documents and answer the questions that follow each document.

DOCUMENT 1

> The Liberator [Simón Bolívar] has energy; he is capable of making a firm decision and sticking to it. His ideas are never commonplace—always large, lofty, and original . . . Glory is his ambition, and his glory consists in having liberated ten million persons and founded three republics . . .
>
> [H]e sometimes appears too dogmatic, and is not always tolerant enough with those who contradict him. He scorns servile flattery and base adulators. He is sensitive to criticism of his actions . . .
>
> [H]e dislikes the poorly educated, the bold, the windbag, the indiscreet, and the discourteous . . . he takes pleasure in criticizing such people . . .
>
> He is a lover of truth, heroism, and honor and of the public interest and morality. He detests and scorns all that is opposed to these . . . sentiments.
>
> —Louis Peru de Lacroix, description of Simón Bolívar, 1828

From "Man of Destiny" (retitled "The Great Liberator") by Louis Peru de Lacroix from *Latin American Civilization: The Colonial Origins*, Vol. 1, Third Edition, edited by Benjamin Keen. Copyright © 1974 by **Benjamin Keen**. Reproduced by permission of the editor.

1. What faults did Lacroix notice in Bolívar's character?

_____

_____

2. Which of Bolívar's personal characteristics helped him as a leader?

_____

_____

Activity 5   Part III: Document-Based Activity

An Age of Revolution

DOCUMENT 2

Before You Read The following document is a song composed by a
French military officer after France declared war on Austria in 1792. It
became widely popular and was later named the French national anthem.

Arise you children of our Motherland!
Oh now is here our glorious day!
Over us the bloodstained banner,
Of tyranny holds sway! (repeat)
Oh do you hear there in our fields
The roar of those fierce fighting men?
Who came right here into our midst
To slaughter sons, wives and kin

To arms, oh citizens!
Form up in serried ranks!
March on, march on!
And drench our fields
With their tainted blood! . . .

Supreme devotion to our Motherland,
Guides and sustains avenging hands
Liberty, oh dearest Liberty,
Come fight with your shieldings bands. (repeat)

—Claude-Joseph Rouget de Lisle, *La Marseillaise*, 1792

3. How does this song justify warfare?

_____

_____

_____

4. How does this song express French nationalism?

_____

_____

_____

Activity 5

Part III: Document-Based Activity

An Age of Revolution

DOCUMENT 3

Before You Read The author of the document below, Camillo Benso, count of Cavour, was a leader of the effort to unify Italy.

> The history of every age proves that no people can attain a high degree of intelligence and morality unless its feeling of nationality is strongly developed. This noteworthy fact is an inevitable consequence of the laws that rule human nature . . . Therefore, if we so ardently desire the emancipation of Italy—if we declare that in the face of this great question all the petty questions that divide us must be silenced—it is not only that we may see our country glorious and powerful but that above all we may elevate her in intelligence and moral development up to the plane of the most civilized nations . . . This union we preach with such ardor is not so difficult to obtain as one might suppose if one judged only by exterior appearances or if one were preoccupied with our unhappy divisions. Nationalism has become general; it grows daily; and it has already grown strong enough to keep all parts of Italy united despite the differences that distinguish them.
>
> —Camillo Benso, count of Cavour, 1846

5. How does the Count of Cavour describe nationalism in Italy?

_____

_____

6. Why does the Count of Cavour believe that Italy should be unified?

_____

_____

Part III: Document-Based Activity

An Age of Revolution

DOCUMENT 4

Before You Read The following words in the document below may be
new to you: *cunning, ingenuousness.* You may want to look them up in a
dictionary.

The first, original, and truly natural boundaries of states are beyond doubt
their internal boundaries. Those who speak the same language are joined to
each other by a multitude of invisible bonds by nature herself, long before
any human art begins; they understand each other and have the power of
continuing to make themselves understood more and more clearly; they
belong together and are by nature one and an inseparable whole. Such a
whole, if it wishes to absorb and mingle with itself any other people of
different descent and language, cannot do so without itself becoming
confused, in the beginning at any rate, and violently disturbing the even
progress of its culture . . .

Thus was the German nation placed—sufficiently united within itself by
a common language and a common way of thinking, and sharply enough
severed from the other peoples—in the middle of Europe . . .

That things should remain thus did not suit the selfishness of foreign
countries, whose calculations did not look more than one moment ahead.
They found German bravery useful in waging their wars and German
hands useful to snatch the booty from their rivals. A means had to be found
to attain this end, and foreign cunning won an easy victory over German
ingenuousness and lack of suspicion . . . [F]oreign countries, I say, made
use of these [religious] disputes to break up the close inner unity of
Germany into separate and disconnected parts.

—Johann Gottlieb Fichte, *Addresses to the German Nation*, 1806

From "Thirteenth Address" by Johann Gottlieb Fichte, from *Addresses to the German Nation*,
edited by George A. Kelly. Copyright © 1968 by George A. Kelly. Reproduced by permission
of **HarperCollins Publishers, Inc.**

7. How does Fichte define the natural boundaries of states?

_____

_____

8. According to Fichte, how did foreign countries affect Germany?

_____

_____

_____

Activity 5   Part III: Document-Based Activity

An Age of Revolution

DOCUMENT 5
Juan O'Gorman, "The Independence Mural," 1960

Before You Read The painting below shows Father Miguel Hidalgo, who in 1810 inspired the Mexican movement for independence from Spain.

Robert Frerck/Odyssey Productions, Inc.

9. According to this painting, who took part in the Mexican movement for independence?

_____

_____

_____

10. How does this painting show Mexican nationalism?

_____

_____

_____

DOCUMENT 6

Before You Read The following words in the document below may be
new to you: *orthodoxy*, *autocracy*, *permeate*. You may want to look them
up in a dictionary.

Without love for the faith of its ancestors, a people, just as an individual, is
bound to perish. A Russian devoted to his country will no more consent to
the loss of one of the tenets of our *Orthodoxy* than to the theft of one pearl
from the crown . . .

Autocracy constitutes the chief condition of the political experience of
Russia . . . The saving conviction that Russia lives and is preserved by the
spirit of a strong, humane, enlightened autocracy must permeate public
education and develop with it.

Beside these two national principles, there is a third, no less important,
no less powerful: *nationality*. The question of nationality does not have the
unity of the preceding one; but both take their origin from the same source
and are linked on every page of the history of the Russian Empire. All the
difficulty concerning nationality consists in harmonizing old and new
conceptions; but nationality does not compel us to go back or stand still; it
does not require immobility in ideas. The government system, as the
human body, must change its aspect with time; features alter with years,
but their character must not alter.

—Russian Minister of Education Sergey Uvarov, report, 1834

From "Orthodoxy, Autocracy, Nationality" from *Life and Thought in Old Russia*, edited by
Marthe Blinoff (University Park, PA, 1961). Copyright © 1961 by **The Pennsylvania State
University Press**. Reproduced by permission of the publisher.

11. What three important principles does Uvarov identify?

_____

_____

_____

12. How does Uvarov's report address nationalism in Russia?

_____

_____

_____

Activity 5

Part III: Document-Based Activity

An Age of Revolution

DOCUMENT 7

Before You Read The document below is taken from a speech given by Irish leader Daniel O'Connell to the British House of Commons, in which O'Connell calls for better treatment for Ireland.

> The question is one in the highest degree interesting to the people of Ireland. It is, whether we mean to do justice to that country—whether we mean to continue the injustice which has been already done to it, or to hold out the hope that it will be treated in the same manner as England and Scotland. That is the question . . .
>
> It has been observed that the object of a king's speech is to say as little in as many words as possible; but this speech contains more things than words—it contains those great principles which, adopted in practice, will be most salutary not only to the British Empire, but to the world . . .
>
> I ask you only for justice: will you—can you—I will not say dare you refuse, because that would make you turn the other way. I implore you, as English gentlemen, to take this matter into consideration now . . . I demand, I respectfully insist: on equal justice for Ireland, on the same principle by which it was been administered to Scotland and England. I will not take less. Refuse me that if you can.
>
> —Daniel O'Connell, speech, February 4, 1836

13. What is O'Connell asking for?

_____

_____

_____

14. What words or ideas does O'Connell use to try to gain support for his request?

_____

_____

_____

Activity 5

Part III: Document-Based Activity

An Age of Revolution

Part B: Writing a Document-Based Essay

HISTORICAL CONTEXT In the 1800s a new spirit of nationalism swept across Europe and the Americas. In Europe, nationalism sparked revolutions and the formation of new nations. In Latin America, colonies won their independence from Europe.

TASK Using information from the documents and your knowledge of world history, write an essay in which you:

- Analyze the causes and effects of nationalism in the countries of Europe and Latin America in the 1800s.

DIRECTIONS Using the information from the documents provided and your knowledge of world history, write a well-organized essay that includes an introduction, a body of several paragraphs, and a conclusion. In the body of the essay, use examples from at least *five* documents. Support your response with relevant facts, examples, and details. Include additional outside information.

GUIDELINES
In your essay, be sure to:

- Address all aspects of the **Task** by accurately analyzing and interpreting at least *five* documents.

- Incorporate information from the documents in the body of the essay.

- Incorporate relevant outside information.

- Support the theme with relevant facts, examples, and details.

- Use a logical and clear plan of organization.

- Introduce the theme by establishing a framework that is beyond a simple statement of the **Task** or **Historical Context**.

- Conclude the essay with a summation of the theme.

Activity 6

Part I: Multiple-Choice Questions

A Half Century of Crisis and Achievement

DIRECTIONS Read each question and circle the number of the best response.

Base your answer to question 1 on the photograph below and on your knowledge of social studies.

1   This poster is an example of which of the following?

   (1) propaganda
   (2) totalitarianism
   (3) genocide
   (4) appeasement

2   During World War I, genocide was committed against

   (1) Jews
   (2) Serbs
   (3) Armenians
   (4) Scandinavians

3   Mohandas Gandhi pushed for India's independence by supporting nonviolent action and

   (1) economic independence
   (2) civil disobedience
   (3) a communist revolution
   (4) totalitarianism

4   Which describes Germany's position for much of World War I?

   (1) All of its military efforts were focused on Serbia.
   (2) It faced war on two fronts.
   (3) It was a neutral country.
   (4) It occupied most of Europe after a series of rapid offensives.

5   Which of these reduced international trade during the Great Depression?

   (1) New Deal
   (2) stock market crash of 1929
   (3) Smoot-Hawley Tariff Act
   (4) Lend-Lease Act

6   Which statement is true about World War I?

   (1) The Battle of Verdun broke the stalemate that had ended trench warfare.
   (2) The Allied Powers were successful in the Gallipoli Campaign.
   (3) The murder of Archduke Franz Ferdinand led to the war's outbreak.
   (4) Woodrow Wilson tried to get the United States to become an imperial power.

Activity 6 Part I: Multiple-Choice Questions

A Half Century of Crisis and Achievement

7 A major turning point in the Pacific theater during World War II was the Battle of

(1) Stalingrad
(2) Midway
(3) El Alamein
(4) the Somme

Base your answer to question 8 on the graph below and on your knowledge of social studies.

Europe's Jewish Population

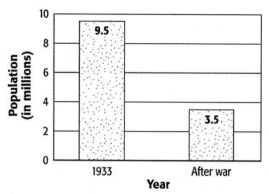

Source: United States Holocaust Memorial Museum

8 This graph illustrates the

(1) migration of European Jews to Israel after World War II
(2) deportation of thousands of German Jews by Nazi Germany
(3) deaths of 6 million Jews worldwide during World War II
(4) decrease in Europe's Jewish population between 1933 and the surrender of Nazi Germany

9 Kemal Ataturk tried to modernize Turkey by

(1) issuing the Balfour Declaration
(2) founding an Islamic state
(3) creating a secular government
(4) forming an alliance with Greece

10 Which event occurred first?

(1) civil war between Bolsheviks and the White Army
(2) the Bolshevik Revolution
(3) Lenin allowing some capitalist activity
(4) Russia entering World War I

11 Which countries were allies during World War II?

(1) Germany and the United States
(2) Japan and the Soviet Union
(3) the United States and Great Britain
(4) Germany and Austria-Hungary

12 One effect of the Great Depression in Germany was

(1) the democratization of Germany
(2) increased support for the Treaty of Versailles
(3) that it was able to pay off its World War I reparations
(4) that many Germans supported the rise of fascism

Activity 6

Part I: Multiple-Choice Questions

A Half Century of Crisis and Achievement

13 The Treaty of Versailles benefited

    (1) India by ending colonialism

    (2) Japan by giving it part of China

    (3) the United States because it joined the League of Nations

    (4) the Soviets because it kept Germany from attacking the Soviet Union

Base your answer to question 14 on the passage below and on your knowledge of social studies.

> "All private ownership of land is abolished immediately without compensation [payment to the owners]. All landowners' estates and all land belonging to the Crown, to monasteries, church lands and all their livestock and . . . property . . . are transferred to the disposition of [control of] the township Land Committees."

14 The passage concerns the political goals of

    (1) Mohandas Gandhi

    (2) Adolf Hitler

    (3) Vladimir Lenin

    (4) Winston Churchill

15 Which Asian country's expansionist foreign policy was *most* likely inspired by European imperialism?

    (1) Japan

    (2) China

    (3) India

    (4) Korea

16 What was one effect of the Balfour Declaration in the Middle East?

    (1) anger about broken promises

    (2) decline in the Jewish population

    (3) creation of a Palestinian state and a Jewish state

    (4) discovery of the world's largest oil fields

17 Which of the following statements about World War II is correct?

    (1) The Soviet Union started the war as an ally of Great Britain.

    (2) The German offensive was based on trench warfare.

    (3) Japan surrendered before Germany.

    (4) Japan first attacked the United States at Pearl Harbor.

Activity 6

Part I: Multiple-Choice Questions

A Half Century of Crisis and Achievement

18 Which new military technology enabled the British to defend London during World War II?

(1) atomic bomb
(2) machine guns
(3) radar
(4) tanks

19 Which factor **least** contributed to the outbreak of World War I?

(1) appeasement
(2) alliances
(3) militarism
(4) nationalism

20 Czar Nicholas II welcomed World War I because he

(1) wanted a chance to defeat the United States
(2) believed in the self-determination of peoples
(3) hoped it would deflect attention from domestic problems
(4) wanted a secret alliance with Mexico

Activity 6

Part II: Thematic Essay

A Half Century of Crisis and Achievement

Answers to the essay questions are to be written on a separate sheet of paper.

In developing your answer to Part II, be sure to keep these general definitions in mind:

(a) *Discuss* means "to make observations about something by using facts, reasoning, and argument; to present in some detail."

(b) *Describe* means "to tell about or to illustrate something in words."

(c) *Explain* means "to make plain or understandable; to give reasons for or causes of; to show the logical development or relationships of"

PART II: THEMATIC ESSAY QUESTION

DIRECTIONS Write a well-organized essay that includes an introduction, several paragraphs addressing the task below, and a conclusion.

THEME Nationalism

> Nationalism is a strong devotion to one's nation or culture. Nationalism has often been a cause of conflict. It has also contributed to the creation of new countries and governments.

TASK Discuss the role of nationalism in the events of World War I, including the lead-up to and the aftermath of the war.

> • Discuss how nationalism contributed to events in the Balkans that helped cause World War I.
>
> • Explain the role of nationalism in the peace negotiations at the end of World War I, which resulted in the Treaty of Versailles.
>
> • Describe the effects of nationalism in *one* country or region in the period between the two world wars.

You may describe the role of nationalism in any country or region. Some suggestions that you might wish to consider include nationalism in Italy, Serbia, Germany, Great Britain, France, and Russia.

You are *not* limited to these suggestions.

GUIDELINES

In your essay, be sure to

- Develop all aspects of the task.
- Support the theme with relevant facts, examples, and details.
- Use a logical and clear plan of organization, including an introduction and a conclusion that are beyond a restatement of the theme.

Activity 6   Part III: Document-Based Activity
A Half Century of Crisis and Achievement

Part A: Using Source Materials

HISTORICAL CONTEXT With the outbreak of fighting in 1939, the world witnessed a war unlike any it had ever seen before. Governments on both sides of World War II took unprecedented steps to mobilize for total war. Axis and Allied countries alike dedicated vast resources to the war effort. Government agencies, civilian industries, and ordinary citizens were united by their common commitment to winning the war.

TASK Using information from the documents and your knowledge of world history, answer the questions that follow each document in Part A. Your answers to the questions will help you write the Part B essay.

DIRECTIONS Examine the following documents and answer the questions that follow each document.

DOCUMENT 1

> How long it [the war] will be, how long it will last, depends upon the exertions which we make in this Island. An effort the like of which has never been seen in our records is now being made. Work is proceeding everywhere, night and day, Sundays and week days. Capital and Labor have cast aside their interests, rights, and customs and put them into the common stock. Already the flow of munitions has leaped forward. There is no reason why we should not in a few months overtake the sudden and serious loss that has come upon us, without retarding the development of our general program.
>
> —British Prime Minister Winston Churchill's speech to the House of Commons, June 4, 1940

1. According to Winston Churchill, what action is the British government taking to mobilize for war?

_____

_____

2. What might have been the purpose of this speech?

_____

_____

Activity 6

Part III: Document-Based Activity

A Half Century of Crisis and Achievement

DOCUMENT 2
"You can help, too!"
German war poster, c. 1941

Library of Congress, LC-USZ62-59940

3. According to the poster, how might women help the war effort?

_____

_____

_____

4. What was likely the purpose of this poster? How can you tell?

_____

_____

_____

Part III: Document-Based Activity

A Half Century of Crisis and Achievement

DOCUMENT 3

> Our task is hard—our task is unprecedented—and the time is short. We must strain every existing armament-producing facility to the utmost. We must convert every available plan and tool to war production. That goes all the way from the greatest plants to the smallest—from the huge automobile industry to the village machine shop.
>
> Production for war is based on men and women—the human hands and brains which collectively we call Labor. Our workers stand ready to work long hours; to turn out more in a day's work; to keep the wheels turning and the fires burning twenty-four hours a day and seven days a week. They realize well that on the speed and efficiency of their work depend the lives of their sons and their brothers on the fighting fronts.
>
> —President Franklin D. Roosevelt, quoted in the U.S. War Production Board's pamphlet *U.S. Labor Goes to War*, published May 1, 1942

5. According to document above, what must the government do to prepare for battle?

_____

_____

_____

6. What role will labor play in the war effort?

_____

_____

_____

Activity 6

Part III: Document-Based Activity

A Half Century of Crisis and Achievement

DOCUMENT 4

> BY VIRTUE Of the authority vested in me by the Constitution and statutes, as President of the United States, and in order to meet the manpower requirements of our armed forces and our expanding war production program by a fuller utilization of our available manpower, it is hereby ordered:
>
> 1. For the duration of the war, no plant, factory, or other place of employment shall be deemed to be making the most effective utilization of its manpower if the minimum work week therein is less than 48 hours per week.
>
> —President Franklin D. Roosevelt's
> Executive Order 9301, issued February 9, 1943

7. What did Executive Order 9301 establish?

_____

_____

_____

8. What effect might Executive Order 9301 have had on the U.S. war effort?

_____

_____

_____

Activity 6   Part III: Document-Based Activity

A Half Century of Crisis and Achievement

DOCUMENT 5

You, my listeners, represent the nation to the world at this moment! And I want to direct ten questions to you, which you along with the German people must answer before the whole world, especially our enemies, who are also listening to us on the radio at this hour! Do you want that? [Enthusiastic shouts: "Yes!"] . . .

Third: The English assert that the German people are no longer willing to undertake the increasing war efforts that the government demands. I ask you: Soldiers and workers, are you and the German people determined, if the Fuhrer should command it in an emergency, to work ten, twelve, if necessary fourteen and sixteen hours daily and to give your all for victory? ["Yes!" Loud applause.] . . .

I ask you, sixth: Are you ready from now on to use all your strength to supply the eastern front, our fighting fathers and brothers, all the men and weapons they need in order to conquer Bolshevism? Are you ready for this? ["Yes!" Loud applause and acclamation.]

I ask you, seventh: Do you swear a sacred vow to the front that the home front stands behind the fighting front with strong, unshakable morale and will give the front everything it needs for victory? ["Yes!" Loud applause.]

I ask you, eighth: Do you, especially you women, want the government to ensure that women, too, make their work available to the war effort [feminine voices: "Yes!"] and that women step in wherever possible to free up men for service on the front? Do you want this? [Loud shouts, especially by women: "Yes!" Loud applause.]

—German propaganda minister Joseph Goebbels's speech on total war, Berlin, Germany, February 18, 1943

---

9. What steps does Goebbels ask the German people to take for the war effort?

_____

_____

_____

10. Why do you think Goebbels gave such a speech in the middle of the war?

_____

_____

_____

Activity 6

Part III: Document-Based Activity

A Half Century of Crisis and Achievement

DOCUMENT 6

The year the Pacific War broke out was the year I entered Yamaguchi Girls' High School . . .

In my first year, we still had classes . . . Later, school classes practically came to an end and our education became mostly volunteer work. Because men were continually going off to the front, we were sent to help their families—planting rice, weeding the paddies, harvesting rice, growing barley. I carried charcoal down from the mountains. I'd had no farm experience before. It was very strenuous, physical labor, but I never thought of it as hardship. We patched soldiers' uniforms, sewed on new buttons, repaired torn seams for the Forty-Second Infantry Regiment stationed in Yamaguchi. Nobody complained about it. We were part of a divine country centered on the Emperor. The whole Japanese race was fighting a war.

In 1944 an army officer from the military arsenal in Kokura on Kyushu came to our school and told us that we would be making a "secret weapon." The weapon would have a great impact on the war. He didn't say then that we were to be making balloon bombs, only that somehow what we made would fly to America. What a sense of mission we had!

—Tanaka Tetsuko, student in Yamaguchi, Japan
from *Japan at War: An Oral History*

Source: Japan at War, an Oral History, Haruko Taya Cook and Theodore F. Cook, eds.
New York: The New Press, 1992

11. Why do you think that Tanaka Tetsuko's education "became mostly volunteer work" after the war began?

_____

_____

_____

12. How did students at the Yamaguchi Girls' High School contribute to the Japanese war effort?

_____

_____

_____

Part III: Document-Based Activity

A Half Century of Crisis and Achievement

DOCUMENT 7

Before the United States officially entered World War II in late 1941, American industry was already busy producing war materials for the Allied forces. However, few employers considered hiring women for factory jobs. Historically it was a common belief that women had no ability to do mechanical or technical jobs. Women and men were expected to fill stereo-typical roles, so two labor markets existed—one for men and one for women. Women were given jobs as secretaries, office clerks, retail clerks, teachers, librarians, and nurses. Black women were relegated to domestic services. Factory jobs were for men only. However, when the United States entered the war and American men joined the military to serve overseas, a monumental attitude change was required. As millions of male workers left the workplace, the resulting labor shortage forced employers to begin hiring women for work traditionally handled by men.

The attitude of many employers changed quickly. Managers, often called foremen, began hiring women for factory jobs and were soon amazed: It was clear to them that women excelled in tasks requiring high degrees of dexterity and speed; women had patience for long-drawn-out jobs far surpassing that of male workers, such as installing complex electrical wiring systems in aircraft; and they were outstanding in production of instruments that required great accuracy in the measurements of components . . .

Walking through any U.S. manufacturing plant in November 1941, a person would have rarely, if ever, seen a woman in the factory rooms. Two years later nearly 35 percent of factory workers were women.

—"Mobilization of Women," from *American Home Front in World War II*

From "Factory work" from "Mobilization of Women" from *American Home Front in World War II*, Vol. 1: *Almanac*, edited by Richard Hanes, Sharon Hanes, and Allison McNeill. Copyright © 2005 by **Thomson Gale, a part of The Thomson Corporation**. Reproduced by permission of the publisher.

13. What jobs did women have before World War II?

_____

_____

14. How did the role of women in the American workforce change during World War II?

_____

_____

_____

Part III: Document-Based Activity

A Half Century of Crisis and Achievement

Part B: Writing a Document-Based Essay

HISTORICAL CONTEXT With the outbreak of fighting in 1939, the world witnessed a war unlike any it had ever seen before. Governments on both sides of World War II took unprecedented steps to mobilize for total war. Axis and Allied countries alike dedicated vast resources to the war effort. Government agencies, civilian industries, and ordinary citizens were united by their common commitment to winning the war.

TASK Using information from the documents and your knowledge of world history, write an essay in which you:

- Describe the actions taken by governments in order to mobilize their countries' resources for war at the beginning of World War II.

- Examine the contributions that citizens on the home front made during World War II.

DIRECTIONS Using the information from the documents provided and your knowledge of world history, write a well-organized essay that includes an introduction, a body of several paragraphs, and a conclusion. In the body of the essay, use examples from at least *five* documents. Support your response with relevant facts, examples, and details. Include additional outside information.

GUIDELINES
In your essay, be sure to:

- Address all aspects of the **Task** by accurately analyzing and interpreting at least *five* documents.

- Incorporate information from the documents in the body of the essay.

- Incorporate relevant outside information.

- Support the theme with relevant facts, examples, and details.

- Use a logical and clear plan of organization.

- Introduce the theme by establishing a framework that is beyond a simple statement of the **Task** or **Historical Context**.

- Conclude the essay with a summation of the theme.

Activity 7

Part I: Multiple-Choice Questions

The 20th Century since 1945

DIRECTIONS Read each question and circle the number of the best response.

Base your answer to question 1 on the map below and on your knowledge of social studies.

The Korean War, 1950–1951

① In a surprise attack, North Korean troops invade the South.

② UN forces land at Inchon attacking behind North Korean lines.

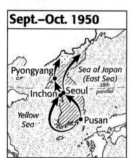

1   What happened in November 1950 when China entered the Korean War on the side of North Korea?

   (1)   UN forces attacked behind South Korean lines.
   (2)   North Korean troops retreated into China.
   (3)   South Korea lost control of territory North of Inchon.
   (4)   North Korea lost control over the city of Pusan.

2   Fidel Castro's goals at the start of the Cuban Revolution included

   (1)   redistributing wealth
   (2)   building a free market economy
   (3)   becoming an ally of the Soviet Union
   (4)   signing the North American Free Trade Agreement

3   The Truman Doctrine *most* contributed to the

   (1)   founding of Solidarity in Poland
   (2)   collapse of European imperialism
   (3)   effort to keep communism from spreading to Korea
   (4)   founding of the United Nations

4   The Marshall Plan laid the foundation for the

   (1)   creation of the Common Market in Europe
   (2)   rapid economic growth of the Pacific Rim countries
   (3)   creation of the Organization of Petroleum Exporting Countries
   (4)   Great Leap Forward and Cultural Revolution in China

Part I: Multiple-Choice Questions

The 20th Century since 1945

5 What was the main cause of the conflict that resulted in the partition of India in 1947?

(1) religious differences
(2) superpower rivalries
(3) Mohandas Gandhi's protest movement
(4) competition for scarce natural resources

6 The Great Leap Forward contributed to China's

(1) having the second largest economy in the world
(2) losing the support of the Soviet Union
(3) providing greater human rights protections
(4) having better relations with the United States

7 At which location did events occur that contributed to both the beginning and the end of the Cold War?

(1) Cuba
(2) West Pakistan
(3) Berlin
(4) Hong Kong

8 During the 1990s, ethnic tensions led to genocide in

(1) China
(2) India
(3) Rwanda
(4) Hungary

9 As a result of the Cold War, political events in Egypt were influenced by

(1) the rivalry between superpowers
(2) increased demand for energy
(3) the Arab-Israeli conflict
(4) the spread of communism to Cuba

10 Juan Perón established himself as a populist in Argentina by gaining the support of

(1) business owners
(2) Marxists
(3) the common people
(4) the United States

11 Which event was a direct effect of the collapse of communism?

(1) ethnic conflict in Bosnia and Kosovo
(2) Persian Gulf War
(3) Sandinista movement in Nicaragua
(4) Korean War

Base your answer to question 12 on the graphic below and on your knowledge of social studies.

GDP per Capita in Latin America

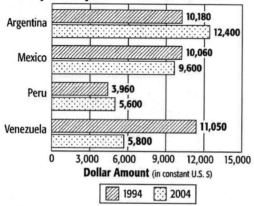

Sources: The World Almanac and Book of Facts, 1997; The World Almanac and Book of Facts, 2006

12 Which of the following statements is best supported by the information in the graph?

(1) All Latin American economies suffered setbacks between 1994 and 2004.
(2) The populations of Latin American countries are growing.
(3) More people in Latin American countries lived below the poverty line in 2004 than in 1994.
(4) In general, the economies of most Latin American countries grew.

13 Which event occurred last in China?

(1) Mao Zedong rises to power.
(2) Government troops kill protestors in Tiananmen Square.
(3) The Cultural Revolution promotes peasants and workers.
(4) China has the second largest economy in the world.

14 One major effect of the Iranian Revolution was that

(1) a more secular society developed
(2) religious fundamentalism grew
(3) market reforms ended
(4) the Communists lost power

15 The rise of the Palestinian Liberation Organization was *least* related to the

(1) Russian Revolution
(2) rise in terrorism
(3) Arab-Israeli wars
(4) rise of nationalism

16 The North American Free Trade Agreement contributed to market reforms in

(1) Poland
(2) Japan
(3) Mexico
(4) Brazil

Activity 7

Part I: Multiple-Choice Questions

The 20th Century since 1945

17 Which Chinese leader introduced the economic policy of limited privatization?

(1) Chiang Kai-shek
(2) Mao Zedong
(3) Deng Xiaoping
(4) Jiang Qing

18 Before gaining independence, Vietnam was a colony of

(1) Great Britain
(2) France
(3) the United States
(4) the Soviet Union

19 To what cause in South Africa was the African National Congress committed to?

(1) ending racial segregation
(2) introducing capitalist land reforms
(3) ending British rule
(4) nonalignment with the superpowers

Base your answer to question 20 on the passage below and on your knowledge of social studies.

"Perestroika is an urgent necessity. . . This society is ripe for change. It has been yearning for it. Any delay in beginning perestroika could [lead] to serious social, economic, and political crises."

—*Perestroika: New Thinking for our Country and the World*, 1987

20 Who made this statement?

(1) Nelson Mandela
(2) Golda Meir
(3) Mao Zedong
(4) Mikhail Gorbachev

Activity 7

Part II: Thematic Essay

The 20th Century since 1945

Answers to the essay questions are to be written on a separate sheet of paper.

In developing your answer to part II, be sure to keep these general definitions in mind:

    (a) *Discuss* means "to make observations about something by using facts, reasoning, and argument; to present in some detail."

    (b) *Describe* means "to tell about or illustrate something in words."

    (c) *Evaluate* means to "examine and judge the significance, worth, or condition of; to determine the value of."

PART II: THEMATIC ESSAY QUESTION

DIRECTIONS Write a well-organized essay that includes an introduction, several paragraphs addressing the task below, and a conclusion.

THEME Political Systems

> After World War II, many countries in Africa and Asia struggled for political and economic independence from European rule. After gaining independence, these nations faced the challenge of building stable governments, economies, and societies.

TASK Identify *two* nations that formed as a result of independence movements and for *each* nation

> • Discuss the historical context that gave rise to its independence movement.
>
> • Describe the key events in that nation's independence movement.
>
> • Evaluate *two* effects or challenges brought about by independence.

You may choose any society from your study of global history. Some suggestions you might wish to consider include the independence movements that led to the formation of the modern nations of India, Vietnam, South Africa, Kenya, and Ghana.

You are *not* limited to these suggestions.

GUIDELINES

In your essay, be sure to

• Develop all aspects of the task.

• Support the theme with relevant facts, examples, and details.

• Use a logical and clear plan of organization, including an introduction and a conclusion that are beyond a restatement of the theme.

Activity 7

Part III: Document-Based Activity

The 20th Century since 1945

Part A: Using Source Materials

HISTORICAL CONTEXT After World War II, the Jewish nationalist movement in Palestine—which had been controlled by Great Britain for over two decades—led to the creation of Israel in 1948. Five Arab nations immediately attacked Israel in what became the first of a series of Arab-Israel wars. Today, the Arab-Israeli conflict continues.

TASK Using information from the documents and your knowledge of world history, answer the questions that follow each document in Part A. Your answers to the questions will help you write the Part B essay.

DIRECTIONS Examine the following documents and answer the questions that follow each document.

DOCUMENT 1

> The Arab case is based upon the fact that Palestine is a country which the Arabs have occupied for more than a thousand years, and a denial of the Jewish historical claims to Palestine. In issuing the Balfour Declaration, the Arabs maintain, the British Government were giving away something that did not belong to Britain . . .
>
> The Arabs of Palestine point out that all the surrounding Arab States have now been granted independence. They argue that they are just as advanced as are the citizens of the nearby States, and they demand independence for Palestine now.
>
> —Anglo-American Committee of Inquiry, report on the situation in Palestine, April 20, 1946

1. According to this passage, what is the basis for the Arab claim to Palestine?

_____

_____

2. What did Palestinian Arabs want?

_____

_____

_____

Activity 7 Part III: Document-Based Activity

The 20th Century since 1945

DOCUMENT 2

We . . . emphatically declare that Palestine is a Holy Land, sacred—to Christian, to Jew and to Moslem alike; and because it is a Holy Land, Palestine is not, and can never become, a land which any race or religion can justly claim as its very own . . .

For another reason, in the light of its long history, and particularly its history of the last thirty years, Palestine cannot be regarded as either a purely Arab or a purely Jewish land.

The Jews have a historic connection with the country. The Jewish National Home, though embodying a minority of the population, is today a reality established under international guarantee. It has a right to continued existence, protection and development.

Yet Palestine is not, and never can be, a purely Jewish land. It lies at the crossroads of the Arab world. Its Arab population, descended from long-time inhabitants of the area, rightly look upon Palestine as their homeland.

It is therefore neither just nor practicable that Palestine should become either an Arab State, in which an Arab majority would control the destiny of a Jewish minority, or a Jewish State, in which a Jewish majority would control that of an Arab minority. In neither case would minority guarantees afford adequate protection for the subordinated group.

—Anglo-American Committee of Inquiry, report on the situation in Palestine, April 20, 1946

3. According to this passage, why can Palestine not be regarded as "a purely Arab or a purely Jewish land"?

_____

_____

_____

4. In this passage, what does the Anglo-American Committee of Inquiry recommend for Palestine?

_____

_____

_____

Activity 7

Part III: Document-Based Activity

The 20th Century since 1945

DOCUMENT 3

Before You Read In the document below, "Eretz-Israel" is a Hebrew term for "land of Israel."

Eretz-Israel was the birthplace of the Jewish people. Here their spiritual, religious and political identity was shaped. Here they first attained to statehood, created cultural values of national and universal significance and gave to the world the eternal Book of Books.

After being forcibly exiled from their land, the people remained faithful to it throughout their Dispersion and never ceased to pray and hope for their return to it and for the restoration in it of their political freedom . . .

The catastrophe which recently befell the Jewish people—the massacre of millions of Jews in Europe—was another clear demonstration of the urgency of solving the problem of its homelessness by re-establishing in Eretz-Israel the Jewish State . . .

Accordingly we, members of the People's Council, representatives of the Jewish community of Eretz-Israel and of the Zionist movement, are here assembled on the day of the termination of the British mandate over Eretz-Israel and, by virtue of our natural and historic right and on the strength of the resolution of the United Nations General Assembly, hereby declare the establishment of a Jewish state in Eretz-Israel, to be known as the state of Israel.

—Declaration of Israel's Independence, May 14, 1948

5. What is the basis of the Jewish claim to Eretz-Israel?

_____

_____

_____

6. How did World War II affect the movement for a Jewish state?

_____

_____

_____

Activity 7

Part III: Document-Based Activity

The 20th Century since 1945

DOCUMENT 4

Article 1: Palestine is the homeland of the Arab Palestinian people; it is an indivisible part of the Arab homeland, and the Palestinian people are an integral part of the Arab nation.

Article 2: Palestine, with the boundaries it had during the British Mandate, is an indivisible territorial unit.

Article 3: The Palestinian Arab people possess the legal right to their homeland and have the right to determine their destiny after achieving the liberation of their country in accordance with their wishes and entirely of their own accord and will . . .

Article 9: Armed struggle is the only way to liberate Palestine . . .The Palestinian Arab people assert their absolute determination and firm resolution to continue their armed struggle and to work for an armed popular revolution for the liberation of their country . . .

Article 19: The partition of Palestine in 1947 and the establishment of the state of Israel are entirely illegal, regardless of the passage of time, because they were contrary to the will of the Palestinian people and to their natural right in their homeland, and inconsistent with the principles embodied in the Charter of the United Nations; particularly the right to self-determination.

—The Palestinian National Charter, July 1-17, 1968

7. Does this document accept or reject the establishment of Israel? Why?

_____

_____

_____

8. How do the creators of this document plan to "liberate Palestine"?

_____

_____

_____

Activity 7   Part III: Document-Based Activity

The 20th Century since 1945

DOCUMENT 5

What is peace for Israel? It means that Israel lives in the region with her Arab neighbors in security and safety. Is that logical? I say yes. It means that Israel lives within its borders, secure against any aggression. Is that logical? And I say yes . . .

As for the Palestine cause, nobody could deny that it is the crux of the entire problem . . .

Conceive with me a peace agreement . . . based on the following points.

Ending the occupation of the Arab territories occupied in 1967.

Achievement of the fundamental rights of the Palestinian people and their right to self-determination, including their right to establish their own state.

The right of all states in the area to live in peace within their boundaries, their secure boundaries, which will be secured and guaranteed through procedures to be agreed upon, which will provide appropriate security to international boundaries in addition to appropriate international guarantees.

Commitment of all states in the region to administer the relations among them in accordance with the objectives and principles of the United Nations Charter. Particularly the principles concerning the nonuse of force and a solution of differences among them by peaceful means.

Ending the state of belligerence in the region.

—Egyptian president Anwar Sadat, address to Israel's legislature,
November 20, 1977

9. What does Sadat believe is the cause of the conflict between Arab nations and Israel?

_____

_____

_____

10. What does Sadat suggest as the main points of a Middle East peace agreement?

_____

_____

_____

_____

DOCUMENT 6

Before You Read In the document below, "PLO" refers to Palestine Liberation Organization, an organization of Palestinian political and guerrilla groups that has generally advocated the use of armed force to replace Israel with a Palestinian state. In 1993 the PLO and Israel reached a tentative peace agreement.

The PLO recognizes the right of the State of Israel to exist in peace and security . . .

The PLO commits itself to the Middle East peace process, and to a peaceful resolution of the conflict between the two sides and declares that all outstanding issues relating to permanent status will be resolved through negotiations.

. . . [T]he PLO renounces the use of terrorism and other acts of violence and will assume responsibility over all PLO elements and personnel in order to assure their compliance, prevent violations and discipline violators.

—PLO chairman Yasser Arafat, letter to Israeli prime minister Yitzhak
Rabin, September 9, 1993

In response to your letter of September 9, 1993, I wish to confirm to you that, in light of the PLO commitments included in your letter, the Government of Israel has decided to recognize the PLO as the representative of the Palestinian people and commence negotiations with the PLO within the Middle East peace process.

—Yitzhak Rabin, letter to Yasser Arafat, September 9, 1993

---

11. What did the PLO agree to do, according to the letter from Arafat to Rabin?

_____

_____

_____

12. What did Israel agree to do, according to the letter from Rabin to Arafat?

_____

_____

_____

Activity 7   Part III: Document-Based Activity

The 20th Century since 1945

DOCUMENT 7
Abu Dis, Israel, December 7, 2004

Before You Read In 2002 Israel began to construct a security barrier to
separate Israel from the West Bank, an Israeli-occupied area where many
Palestinians live.

© Jim Hollander/epa/Corbis

13. Why might Israel have begun to construct this barrier?

_____

_____

_____

14. How do you think Palestinians reacted to the barrier?

_____

_____

_____

Activity 7

Part III: Document-Based Activity

The 20th Century since 1945

Part B: Writing a Document-Based Essay

HISTORICAL CONTEXT After World War II, the Jewish nationalist movement in Palestine—which had been controlled by Great Britain for over two decades—led to the creation of Israel in 1948. Five Arab nations immediately attacked Israel in what became the first of a series of Arab-Israel wars. Today, the Arab-Israeli conflict continues.

TASK Using information from the documents and your knowledge of world history, write an essay in which you:

- Discuss the causes of the Arab-Israeli conflict from 1948 to the present.

DIRECTIONS Using the information from the documents provided and your knowledge of world history, write a well-organized essay that includes an introduction, a body of several paragraphs, and a conclusion. In the body of the essay, use examples from at least *five* documents. Support your response with relevant facts, examples, and details. Include additional outside information.

GUIDELINES
In your essay, be sure to:

- Address all aspects of the **Task** by accurately analyzing and interpreting at least *five* documents.

- Incorporate information from the documents in the body of the essay.

- Incorporate relevant outside information.

- Support the theme with relevant facts, examples, and details.

- Use a logical and clear plan of organization.

- Introduce the theme by establishing a framework that is beyond a simple statement of the **Task** or **Historical Context**.

- Conclude the essay with a summation of the theme.

Activity 8

Part I: Multiple-Choice Questions

Global Connections and Interactions

DIRECTIONS Read each question and circle the number of the best response.

Base your answer to question 1 on the chart below and on your knowledge of social studies.

Developed Countries	Developing Countries
• strong economies	• less-productive economies
• industry and technology-based economies	• agricultural based economies
• many educational opportunities	• fewer educational opportunities
• many health care options	• poor health care options

1   Which phrase best describes life in developing countries?

(1) insufficient health care facilities
(2) very little poverty
(3) widespread industrialization
(4) many educational opportunities

2   One main cause of economic interdependence is that

(1) nations are increasingly self-sufficient
(2) economic resources vary from place to place
(3) nations are trying to preserve their cultural traditions
(4) the supply of goods now exceeds demand

3   Outsourcing benefits multinational corporations by

(1) decreasing production
(2) eliminating competition
(3) increasing material costs
(4) cutting labor costs

4   Critics of globalization argue that the process

(1) favors environmental protection over economic growth
(2) benefits developed nations at the expense of developing nations
(3) raises prices for consumer goods
(4) decreases terrorism

5   Why is it difficult to control nuclear proliferation?

(1) Nuclear weapons are very difficult to build.
(2) Nuclear technology is inexpensive.
(3) Many nations use nuclear technology for energy purposes.
(4) There are no agreements regulating the use of nuclear technology.

6   In West Africa desertification is caused by

(1) pollution and hunting
(2) drought and deforestation
(3) industrialization and trade
(4) mining and migration

Activity 8   Part I: Multiple-Choice Questions
Global Connections and Interactions

Base your answer to question 7 on the diagram below and on your knowledge of social studies.

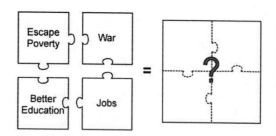

7   Which phrase best completes this diagram?

(1) Technological Advances
(2) Effects of Urbanization
(3) Factors Causing Global Population Movement
(4) Arguments Favoring Globalization

8   One cause of poverty is

(1) the Helsinki Accords
(2) inadequate resources
(3) NGOs
(4) medical advances

9   One benefit of space exploration is

(1) independent economies
(2) less cultural diffusion
(3) the end of the digital divide
(4) new consumer products

10   Which change is **least** associated with a society undergoing the process of modernization?

(1) secularization of the political system
(2) increased respect for customs and traditions
(3) urbanization
(4) changes in women's roles

11   Which is the **best** example of the impact of the Internet?

(1) cultural diffusion
(2) free trade
(3) resource conservation
(4) population growth

12   One effect of international travel is

(1) a greater threat of global disease epidemics
(2) less concern about the effect of cultural diffusion on traditional societies
(3) a decline in service industries like tourism
(4) more concern about illegal immigration

Activity 8   Part I: Multiple-Choice Questions

Global Connections and Interactions

Base your answer to question 13 on the passages below and on your knowledge of social studies.

> "Inequality is growing, but poverty is going down . . . The last twenty years of growth has made more people get out of poverty than at any time in history."
>
> —Meghnad Desai
> economist, 2001

> "And you see it in the streets of every city in the world . . . The rich are getting richer . . . and then the poor, the people at the bottom of the barrel . . . seem to be getting poorer . . . I suggest we get realistic and we acknowledge the undoubted fact that globalization is very good for the rich and very bad for the poor"
>
> —Leslie Sklair
> sociologist, 2001

13 Over which issue related to globalization do the authors disagree?
   (1) the speed at which globalization occurs
   (2) how globalization affects the poor
   (3) technological improvements in transportation
   (4) changing patterns of migration

14 In developing nations, the digital divide is an obstacle to
   (1) urbanization
   (2) economic growth
   (3) treating infectious diseases
   (4) global migration

15 Today, the green revolution is an attempt by agricultural scientists to
   (1) stop the genetic engineering of food crops
   (2) increase the world's food production
   (3) end global warming
   (4) reverse the effects of sustainable development

16 Recent conflicts in Northern Ireland, Bosnia and Herzegovina, Rwanda, and Sudan have been a result of
   (1) inadequate resources
   (2) ethnic differences
   (3) deforestation
   (4) secularization

17 Which of the following is an environmental challenge facing the world's people and places?
   (1) reducing environmental interdependence
   (2) protecting developing nations from trade barriers
   (3) balancing the protection of resources with economic development
   (4) decreasing temperatures that are cooling Earth's climate

18 The world regions with the *fewest* developed nations are

(1) the Middle East and India
(2) the Pacific Rim and eastern Europe
(3) South America and the Caribbean
(4) southern Asia and Africa

19 Which of the following terms describes economic growth that avoids permanent damage to resources?

(1) endangered species
(2) sustainable development
(3) economic sanction
(4) command economy

20 Which organization issued the Universal Declaration of Human Rights?

(1) United Nations
(2) World Trade Organization
(3) International Red Cross
(4) European Union

Activity 8

Part II: Thematic Essay

Global Connections and Interactions

Answers to the essay questions are to be written on a separate sheet of paper.

In developing your answer to Part II, be sure to keep these general definitions in mind:

(a) *Discuss* means "to make observations about something by using facts, reasoning, and argument; to present in some detail."

(b) *Describe* means "to tell about or to illustrate something in words."

(c) *Evaluate* means "to examine and judge the significance, worth, or condition of; to determine the value of."

PART II: THEMATIC ESSAY QUESTION

DIRECTIONS Write a well-organized essay that includes an introduction, several paragraphs addressing the task below, and a conclusion.

THEME Interdependence

Interdependence is a relationship among countries in which they depend on one another for resources, goods, and services. Increased interdependence today is a result of globalization—which is the process by which trade and communication connect the countries of the world.

TASK Evaluate the benefits and costs of globalization.

- Describe the economic and technological causes of globalization.
- Discuss **two** benefits of globalization.
- Discuss **two** costs of globalization.

You may choose any example from your study of global history and geography. Some areas you may want consider are globalization's impact on a region's standard of living and traditional cultures.

You are *not* limited to these suggestions.

GUIDELINES

In your essay, be sure to

- Develop all aspects of the task.
- Support the theme with relevant facts, examples, and details.
- Use a logical and clear plan of organization, including an introduction and a conclusion that are beyond a restatement of the theme.

Activity 8

Part III: Document-Based Activity

Global Connections and Interactions

Part A: Using Source Materials

HISTORICAL CONTEXT The world today is changing rapidly.
Economic development and advances in transportation and
communications technology have helped link together the people of the
world, but globalization has also brought new challenges.

TASK Using information from the documents and your knowledge of
world history; answer the questions that follow each document in Part A.
Your answers to the questions will help you write the Part B essay.

DIRECTIONS Examine the following documents and answer the
questions that follow each document.

DOCUMENT 1

> The majority of agricultural scientists, including myself, anticipate great
> benefits from biotechnology in the coming decades to help meet our future
> needs for food and fiber . . .
>
> We cannot turn back the clock on agriculture and only use methods that
> were developed to feed a much smaller population. It took some 10,000
> years to expand food production to the current level of about 5 billion tons
> per year. By 2025, we will have to nearly double current production again.
> This increase cannot be accomplished unless farmers across the world have
> access to current high-yielding crop production methods as well as new
> biotechnological breakthroughs that can increase the yields, dependability,
> and nutritional quality of our basic food crops.
>
> —Norman E. Borlaug, "Ending World Hunger," *Plant Physiology*,
> October 2000

From "Ending World Hunger: The Promise of Biotechnology and the Threat of Antiscience
Zealotry" by Norman E. Borlaug from *Plant Physiology* web site, October 2000, Vol. 124,
accessed November 29, 2006 at www.plantphysiol.org/cgi/content/full/124/2/987. Copyright
© 2000 by **American Society of Plant Physiologists**. Reproduced by permission of the
publisher.

1. What problem does Borlaug discuss in this passage?

_____

_____

2. How does he suggest solving this problem?

_____

Activity 8
Part III: Document-Based Activity
Global Connections and Interactions

DOCUMENT 2

Before You Read The following words in the document below may be new to you: *anachronism, avant-garde.* You may want to look them up in a dictionary.

I recall with anguish a lecture I heard at Cambridge a few years ago. It was entitled "Literacy Is Doomed," and its thesis was that the alphabetic culture, the one based on writing and books, is perishing. According to the lecturer, audio-visual culture will soon replace it. The written word, and whatever it represents, are already an anachronism since the more avant-garde and urgent knowledge required for the experience of our time is transmitted and stored not in books but in machines and has signals and not letters as its tools.

The lecturer had spent two weeks in Mexico where he had traveled everywhere, and even in the underground [subway system] he had no difficulty, though he spoke no Spanish, because the entire system of instructions in the Mexican underground consists of nothing but arrows, lights, and figures . . .

The lecturer maintained that all Third World countries, instead of persisting in those costly campaigns aimed at teaching their illiterate masses how to read and write, should introduce them to what will be the primary source of knowledge: the handling of machines . . .

It is true that for many people the written word is becoming more and more dispensable . . .

We must be appalled at this, because although I doubt the prophecy . . . will come true, if it does it will be a disaster for humanity.

—Mario Vargas Llosa, "Books, Gadgets, and Freedom," 1987

From "Books, Gadgets, and Freedom" by Mario Vargas Llosa from *The Wilson Quarterly*, Spring 1987. Copyright © 1987 by **Mario Vargas Llosa**. Reproduced by permission of the author.

3. What does the lecturer predict will happen to the written word?

_____

_____

4. According to the lecturer, what should countries do instead of teaching illiterate people how to read and write?

_____

_____

Part III: Document-Based Activity

Global Connections and Interactions

DOCUMENT 3

Before You Read The Group of Eight (G-8) is an organization of eight major industrial democracies that meets regularly to discuss international economic, environmental, and other issues.

> When the Group of Eight (G-8) summit was held last month, the centre of Genoa, [Italy,] where the summit was held, was turned into an armed ghost town, ringed with high fences, barbed wire and shipping containers. Tens of thousands of anti-globalization protesters engaged in violent demonstrations over the three days of meetings . . .
>
> Among these protesters were mainly anti-globalizationists, environmental-protection advocates and labour union activists, who all believe that globalization—characterized by "free trade," "free flow of capital" and international corporate activities—has benefited only the rich, deprived the poor and caused the environment to deteriorate . . .
>
> As enthusiasm grows for the information superhighway, villages and slums in poor countries remain without telephones, electricity or safe water, and there are primary schools without pencils, paper or books. For poor people, the information technology (IT) promises remain as remote as a distant star . . .
>
> Worst of all, the deterioration of [the] global environment is continuing at an unprecedented speed, while the political and financial structure of the world economy, which has become increasingly dominated by powerful multinational corporations, is directly at odds with efforts to promote a healthy earth.
>
> —*China Daily*, "Globalization a lingering dilemma," August 22, 2001

From "Globalization a lingering dilemma" from *China Daily*, August 22, 2001. Copyright © 2001 by **China Daily**. Reproduced by permission of the publisher.

5. At the G-8 summit, what did anti-globalization protestors believe?

_____

_____

_____

6. According to this passage, what is the condition of the global environment?

_____

_____

_____

Activity 8

Part III: Document-Based Activity

Global Connections and Interactions

DOCUMENT 4

The World Trade Organization (WTO) is the only international organization dealing with the global rules of trade between nations. Its main function is to ensure that trade flows as smoothly, predictably and freely as possible.

The result is assurance. Consumers and producers know that they can enjoy secure supplies and greater choice of the finished products, components, raw materials and services that they use. Producers and exporters know that foreign markets will remain open to them.

The result is also a more prosperous, peaceful and accountable economic world. Virtually all decisions in the WTO are taken by consensus among all member countries and they are ratified by members' parliaments. Trade friction is channelled into the WTO's dispute settlement process where the focus is on interpreting agreements and commitments, and how to ensure that countries' trade policies conform with them. That way, the risk of disputes spilling over into political or military conflict is reduced.

By lowering trade barriers, the WTO's system also breaks down other barriers between peoples and nations . . .

The goal is to improve the welfare of the peoples of the member countries.

—www.wto.org, "The WTO . . . In brief," 2006

From "The WTO . . . In brief" from *World Trade Organization* web site accessed November 1, 2006 at www.wto.org/English/thewto_e/whatis_e/inbrief_e/inbro00_e.htm. Copyright © 2006 by **World Trade Organization**.. Reproduced by permission of the publisher.

7. According to this passage, what are the functions and goals of the World Trade Organization (WTO)?

_____

_____

_____

8. Does this passage view the effects of the WTO as positive or negative? Why might the passage take this position?

_____

_____

_____

DOCUMENT 5
Anti-World Trade Organization (WTO) Protestors, the Philippines
December 13, 2005

© Cheryl Ravelo/Reuters/Corbis

9. What are the people in this photograph doing?

_____

_____

_____

10. Why do you think these people oppose the WTO?

_____

_____

_____

Activity 8

Part III: Document-Based Activity

Global Connections and Interactions

DOCUMENT 6

Nearly half of all people now live in cities; an increasing number of them travel enormous distances every year by private car and in aircraft. In the developed world, technology has transformed patterns of work and family life, communications, leisure activities, diet and health. Similar transformations are under way in the more prosperous parts of the developing world.

The impacts of these changes on the natural environment are complex. The modern industrial economies of North America, Europe and parts of East Asia consume immense quantities of energy and raw materials, and produce high volumes of wastes and polluting emissions. The magnitude of this economic activity is causing environmental damage on a global scale and widespread pollution and disruption of ecosystems.

In other regions, particularly in many parts of the developing world, poverty combined with rapid population growth is leading to widespread degradation of renewable resources—primarily forests, soils and water . . . Renewable resources still sustain the livelihood of nearly one-third of the world's population; environmental deterioration therefore directly reduces living standards and prospects for economic improvement among rural peoples. At the same time, rapid urbanization and industrialization in many developing countries are creating high levels of air and water pollution, which often hit the poor hardest. Worldwide, the urban poor tend to live in neglected neighbourhoods, enduring pollution, waste dumping and ill health, but lacking the political influence to effect improvements.

—United Nations Environment Programme, *Global Environment Outlook 2000*, 1999

From "Global perspectives" from *Global Environment Outlook 2000*. Copyright © 1999 by **United Nations Environment Programme**. Reproduced by permission of the publisher.

11. According to the passage, what changes are taking place in the world today?

_____

_____

_____

12. What are the effects of these changes on the natural environment?

_____

_____

Activity 8   Part III: Document-Based Activity

Global Connections and Interactions

DOCUMENT 7

Before You Read The second passage below refers to the World Economic
Forum, an organization of international business leaders and politicians.

> I believe that globalization has benefited people living in developing
> countries in three important ways.
>
> Firstly, opening up markets increases economic growth, which in turn
> improves living standards. Secondly, globalization leads to cheaper
> imports meaning poorer countries pay less for goods they cannot produce.
> Thirdly, it helps undermine totalitarian and corrupt regimes by encouraging
> good practice based on rules.
>
> —Philippe Legrain, BBC News Online, January 16, 2004
>
> I would argue that globalization makes economic and social changes based
> on profit for the few, not the majority of people. In South Africa, the rich
> are getting richer and the poor are getting poorer . . .
>
> My message to the delegates attending the World Economic Forum is
> that your vision of the future is lacking in humanity.
>
> . . . [T]here is a groundswell of people around the world who reject your
> policies—you need to wake up and smell the coffee.
>
> —Trevor Ngwane, BBC News Online, January 16, 2004

From "Head to Head: Social vs economic forum" with Philippe Legrain and Trevor Ngwane
from *BBC News* web site, January 16, 2004, accessed November 2, 2006 at news.bbc.co.uk/
go/pr/fr/-/1/hi/business/3400945.stm. Copyright © 2004 by BBC. Reproduced by permission of
BBC News.

13. According to Legrain, how has globalization benefited people in developing
    countries?

    _____

    _____

    _____

14. Why does Ngwane oppose globalization?

    _____

    _____

    _____

Activity 8 | Part III: Document-Based Activity

Global Connections and Interactions

Part B: Writing a Document-Based Essay

HISTORICAL CONTEXT The world today is changing rapidly. Economic development and advances in transportation and communications technology have helped link together the people of the world, but globalization has also brought new challenges.

TASK Using information from the documents and your knowledge of world history, write an essay in which you:

- Identify the ways in which globalization affects the economies, cultures, and environments of countries around the world today.

- Evaluate different perspectives on globalization.

DIRECTIONS Using the information from the documents provided and your knowledge of world history, write a well-organized essay that includes an introduction, a body of several paragraphs, and a conclusion. In the body of the essay, use examples from at least *five* documents. Support your response with relevant facts, examples, and details. Include additional outside information.

GUIDELINES
In your essay, be sure to:

- Address all aspects of the **Task** by accurately analyzing and interpreting at least *five* documents.

- Incorporate information from the documents in the body of the essay.

- Incorporate relevant outside information.

- Support the theme with relevant facts, examples, and details.

- Use a logical and clear plan of organization.

- Introduce the theme by establishing a framework that is beyond a simple statement of the **Task** or **Historical Context**.

- Conclude the essay with a summation of the theme.

The University of the State of New York

REGENTS HIGH SCHOOL EXAMINATION

GLOBAL HISTORY AND GEOGRAPHY

Wednesday, August 16, 2006 — 12:30 to 3:30 p.m., only

Student Name _____

School Name _____

Print your name and the name of your school on the lines above. Then turn to the last page of this booklet, which is the answer sheet for Part I. Fold the last page along the perforations and, slowly and carefully, tear off the answer sheet. Then fill in the heading of your answer sheet. Now print your name and the name of your school in the heading of each page of your essay booklet.

This examination has three parts. You are to answer **all** questions in all parts. Use black or dark-blue ink to write your answers.

Part I contains 50 multiple-choice questions. Record your answers to these questions on the separate answer sheet.

Part II contains one thematic essay question. Write your answer to this question in the essay booklet, beginning on page 1.

Part III is based on several documents:

Part III A contains the documents. Each document is followed by one or more questions. In the test booklet, write your answer to each question on the lines following that question. Be sure to enter your name and the name of your school on the first page of this section.

Part III B contains one essay question based on the documents. Write your answer to this question in the essay booklet, beginning on page 7.

When you have completed the examination, you must sign the statement printed on the Part I answer sheet, indicating that you had no unlawful knowledge of the questions or answers prior to the examination and that you have neither given nor received assistance in answering any of the questions during the examination. Your answer sheet cannot be accepted if you fail to sign this declaration.

The use of any communications device is strictly prohibited when taking this examination. If you use any communications device, no matter how briefly, your examination will be invalidated and no score will be calculated for you.

DO NOT OPEN THIS EXAMINATION BOOKLET UNTIL THE SIGNAL IS GIVEN.

Part I

Answer all questions in this part.

Directions (1–50): For each statement or question, write on the separate answer sheet the *number* of the word or expression that, of those given, best completes the statement or answers the question.

1 • Height above sea level
  • Distance from the equator
  • Amount of rainfall
  • Average daily temperature

Which aspect of geography is most influenced by these factors?

(1) natural boundaries
(2) climate
(3) topography
(4) mineral resources

2 Which activity would be most characteristic of people in a traditional society?

(1) serving in government assemblies
(2) working in an industrialized city
(3) having the same occupation as their parents
(4) establishing a mercantile system of trade

3 • Large areas in the north and south received less than ten inches of rainfall annually.
  • The presence of waterfalls and rapids slowed river travel.
  • Highlands and steep cliffs limited exploration.

In which region did these geographic factors have an impact on European exploration and colonization?

(1) South America
(2) Southeast Asia
(3) subcontinent of India
(4) Africa

4 What is the main reason the Neolithic Revolution is considered a turning point in world history?

(1) Fire was used as a source of energy for the first time.
(2) Spoken language was used to improve communication.
(3) Domestication of animals and cultivation of crops led to settled communities.
(4) Stone tools and weapons were first developed.

5 Which heading best completes the partial outline below?

I. _____

   A. Centralized governments
   B. Organized religions
   C. Social classes
   D. Specialization of labor

(1) Economic Development in Ancient Egypt
(2) Cultural Diffusion in Mohenjo-Daro
(3) Features of the Old Stone Age
(4) Characteristics of Civilizations

6 The Pillars of Emperor Asoka of the Mauryan Empire and the Code of Hammurabi of Babylon are most similar to the

(1) ziggurats of Sumeria
(2) map projections of Mercator
(3) Great Sphinx of the Egyptians
(4) Twelve Tables of the Romans

7 A similarity between Bantu migrations in Africa and migrations of the ancient Aryans into South Asia is that both moved

(1) across the Atlantic Ocean
(2) from rural lands to urban areas
(3) in search of additional food sources
(4) for religious freedom

8 Which factor led to the development of civilizations in ancient Mesopotamia?

(1) political harmony
(2) favorable geography
(3) religious differences
(4) universal education

9 Which statement most likely represents the view of a citizen of ancient Athens visiting Sparta?

(1) "The government and society in Sparta are so strict. The people have little voice in government."
(2) "I feel as though I have never left home. Everything here is the same as it is in Athens."
(3) "This society allows for more freedom of expression than I have ever experienced in Athens."
(4) "I have never heard of a society like Sparta that believes in only one God."

10 One similarity between animism and Shinto is that people who follow these belief systems

(1) practice filial piety
(2) worship spirits in nature
(3) are monotheistic
(4) are required to make pilgrimages

11 • Buddhist temples are found in Japan.
• Most Indonesians study the Koran.
• Catholicism is the dominant religion in Latin America.

These statements illustrate a result of

(1) westernization
(2) cultural diffusion
(3) economic nationalism
(4) fundamentalism

12 Which group introduced the Cyrillic alphabet, Orthodox Christianity, and domed architecture to Russian culture?

(1) Mongols   (3) Jews
(2) Vikings   (4) Byzantines

13 The topography and climate of Russia have caused Russia to

(1) depend on rice as its main source of food
(2) seek access to warm-water ports
(3) adopt policies of neutrality and isolation
(4) acquire mineral-rich colonies on other continents

14 One of the major achievements of Byzantine Emperor Justinian was that he

(1) established a direct trade route with Ghana
(2) defended the empire against the spread of Islam
(3) brought Roman Catholicism to his empire
(4) preserved and transmitted Greek and Roman culture

15 Both European medieval knights and Japanese samurai warriors pledged oaths of

(1) loyalty to their military leader
(2) devotion to their nation-state
(3) service to their church
(4) allegiance to their families

16 What was a significant effect of Mansa Musa's pilgrimage to Mecca?

(1) The African written language spread to southwest Asia.
(2) Military leaders eventually controlled Mali.
(3) Islamic learning and culture expanded in Mali.
(4) The trading of gold for salt ended.

17 A direct impact that the printing press had on 16th-century Europe was that it encouraged the

(1) spread of ideas
(2) beginnings of communism
(3) establishment of democracy
(4) development of industrialization

18 Which technological advancement helped unify both the Roman and the Inca Empires?

(1) astrolabe   (3) gunpowder
(2) road system   (4) wheeled carts

19 Cervantes' literary classic *Don Quixote*, the rule of Isabella and Ferdinand, and the art of El Greco are associated with the

(1) Golden Age in Spain
(2) Hanseatic League in Germany
(3) Glorious Revolution in England
(4) Renaissance in Italy

Base your answer to question 20 on the diagram below and on your knowledge of social studies.

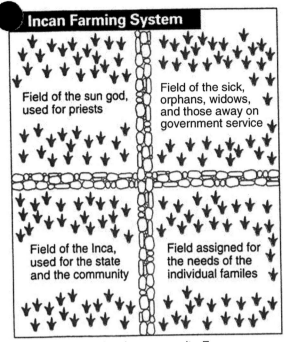

Incan Farming System

Field of the sun god, used for priests

Field of the sick, orphans, widows, and those away on government service

Field of the Inca, used for the state and the community

Field assigned for the needs of the individual families

All land belonged to the community. Farmers grew crops in different fields.

Source: Ellis and Esler, *World History: Connections to Today*, Prentice Hall (adapted)

20 This diagram shows the Incas had a farming system that
(1) provided crops for the entire society
(2) left much of the land unfarmed
(3) set aside fifty percent of the crops for those who farmed the fields
(4) grew crops only for priests and government officials

21 Which statement best describes a result of the encounter between Europeans and native populations of Latin America?
(1) Native societies experienced rapid population growth.
(2) European nations lost power and prestige in the New World.
(3) Large numbers of natives migrated to Europe for a better life.
(4) Plantations in the New World used enslaved Africans to replace native populations.

Base your answers to questions 22 through 24 on the speakers' statements below and on your knowledge of social studies.

Speaker A: Although I spread serfdom in my country, I tried to modernize our society by incorporating western technology.

Speaker B: I promoted culture with my support of the arts. Unfortunately, I drained my country's treasury by building my palace at Versailles and involving my country in costly wars.

Speaker C: I gained much wealth from my overseas empire in the Americas. I waged war against the Protestants and lost.

Speaker D: I inherited the throne and imprisoned my foes without a trial. I dissolved Parliament because I did not want to consult with them when I increased taxes.

22 Which speaker represents the view of King Louis XIV of France?
(1) A   (3) C
(2) B   (4) D

23 Which nation was most likely governed by *Speaker D*?
(1) Russia   (3) Spain
(2) France   (4) England

24 Which type of government is most closely associated with all these speakers?
(1) limited monarchy
(2) absolute monarchy
(3) direct democracy
(4) constitutional democracy

Base your answer to question 25 on the statements below and on your knowledge of social studies.

. . . The Laws ought to be so framed, as to secure the Safety of every Citizen as much as possible.

. . . The Equality of the Citizens consists in this; that they should all be subject to the same Laws. . . .

— *Documents of Catherine the Great*, W. F. Reddaway, ed., Cambridge University Press (adapted)

25 These ideas of Catherine the Great of Russia originated during the

(1) Age of Exploration
(2) Age of Enlightenment
(3) Protestant Reformation
(4) French Revolution

Base your answers to questions 26 and 27 on the speakers' statements below and on your knowledge of social studies.

Speaker A: Government should not interfere in relations between workers and business owners.

Speaker B: The workers will rise up and overthrow the privileged class.

Speaker C: Private property will cease to exist. The people will own the means of production.

Speaker D: A favorable balance of trade should be maintained by the use of tariffs.

26 Which two speakers represent Karl Marx's ideas of communism?

(1) *A* and *B*   (3) *B* and *D*
(2) *B* and *C*   (4) *C* and *D*

27 Which speaker is referring to laissez-faire capitalism?

(1) *A*   (3) *C*
(2) *B*   (4) *D*

Base your answers to questions 28 and 29 on the map below and on your knowledge of social studies.

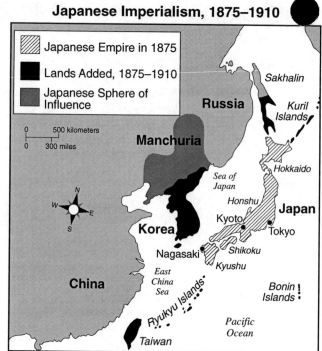

Japanese Imperialism, 1875–1910

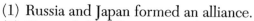

Source: Henry Brun et al., *Reviewing Global History and Geography*, AMSCO (adapted)

28 What was a basic cause of the political changes shown on this map?

(1) Russia and Japan formed an alliance.
(2) Korea defeated Japan in the Sino-Japanese War.
(3) The Japanese people wanted to spread the beliefs of Shinto.
(4) Japan needed raw materials for industrialization.

29 Which event is associated with the changes shown on this map?

(1) Opium War
(2) Meiji Restoration
(3) Chinese Nationalist Revolution
(4) rise of the Soviet Union

30 The Bolshevik Party in 1917 gained the support of the peasant class because they promised them

(1) "Peace, Land, and Bread"
(2) "Liberty, Equality, Fraternity"
(3) abolition of the secret police
(4) democratic reforms in all levels of government

Base your answer to question 31 on the map below and on your knowledge of social studies.

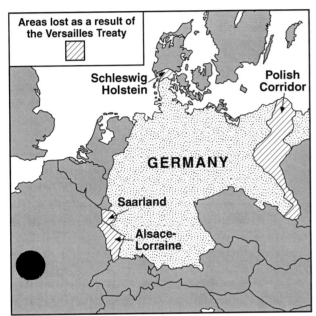

Areas lost as a result of the Versailles Treaty

Schleswig Holstein

Polish Corridor

GERMANY

Saarland

Alsace-Lorraine

Source: Geoffrey Barraclough, ed., *Hammond Concise Atlas of World History*, Hammond, 1998 (adapted)

31 Which time period in German history is most accurately represented in this map?

(1) between World War I and World War II
(2) just after the Berlin Conference
(3) immediately after the Congress of Vienna
(4) during unification under Bismarck

32 Which statement describes one major aspect of a command economy?

(1) Supply and demand determines what will be produced.
(2) Most economic decisions are made by the government.
(3) The means of production are controlled by labor unions.
(4) The economy is mainly agricultural.

33 Which area was once controlled by Britain, suffered a mass starvation in the 1840s, and became an independent Catholic nation in 1922?

(1) Scotland   (3) Ghana
(2) India   (4) Ireland

34 Totalitarian countries are characterized by

(1) free and open discussions of ideas
(2) a multiparty system with several candidates for each office
(3) government control of newspapers, radio, and television
(4) government protection of people's civil liberties

35 Which name would best complete this partial outline?

I. African Nationalists of the 20th Century
   A. Leopold Senghor
   B. Jomo Kenyatta
   C. Julius Nyerere
   D. _____

(1) Atatürk [Mustafa Kemal]
(2) Ho Chi Minh
(3) José de San Martín
(4) Kwame Nkrumah

36 Since 1948, a major reason for the conflict between Arabs and Israelis is that each side

(1) wants the huge oil reserves that lie under the disputed land
(2) believes that the United States favors the other side in the conflict
(3) claims sovereignty over the same land
(4) seeks to control trade on the eastern end of the Mediterranean Sea

37 In the 1980s, Mikhail Gorbachev's attempts to change the Soviet Union resulted in

(1) an increase in tensions between India and the Soviet Union
(2) a strengthening of the Communist Party
(3) a shift from producing consumer goods to producing heavy machinery
(4) a series of economic and political reforms

Base your answer to question 38 on the diagram below and on your knowledge of social studies.

Cycle of the Ecological Environment

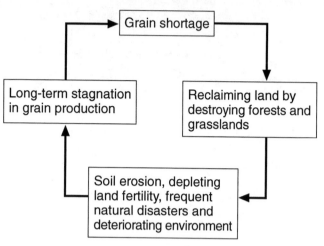

Source: Yan Ruizhen and Wang Yuan, *Poverty and Development*, New World Press, 1992 (adapted)

38 Which conclusion based on the ecological cycle shown in this diagram is most valid?

(1) Grain yields increase as the amount of land reclaimed increases.
(2) The destruction of forests leads to soil erosion.
(3) Grain production has no impact on the environment.
(4) Natural disasters have little effect on grain production.

39 • Egypt builds the Aswan Dam to control flooding and produce hydroelectric power.
• China builds the Three Gorges Dam to control flooding and improve trade.
• Brazil builds the Tucuruí Dam in the tropical rain forest to produce hydroelectric power.

Which conclusion can be drawn from these statements?

(1) Societies often modify their environment to meet their needs.
(2) Monsoons are needed for the development of societies.
(3) Topography creates challenges that societies are unable to overcome.
(4) Land features influence the development of diverse belief systems.

Base your answer to question 40 on the cartoon below and on your knowledge of social studies.

Ziraldo/Rio de Janeiro, Brazil
Cartoonists & Writers Syndicate
Source: Ziraldo Alves Pinto

40 What is the main idea of this Brazilian cartoon?

(1) Relations between Latin America and the United States are mutually beneficial.
(2) The United States wants to cut off political and economic relations with Latin America.
(3) Latin American nations are self-sufficient and need not rely on the United States.
(4) The United States wants to control its relationships with Latin America.

41 **"Tensions Increase Over Kashmir"**
"Hindus and Muslims Clash in Calcutta Riots"
"Threat of Nuclear Conflict Worries World"

These headlines refer to events in which region?

(1) Latin America
(2) sub-Saharan Africa
(3) subcontinent of India
(4) East Asia

Base your answer to question 42 on the cartoon below and on your knowledge of social studies.

Source: Kim Song Heng, *Lianhe Zaobao,* 2002 (adapted)

42 The main idea of this 2002 cartoon is that East Timor is

(1) experiencing massive floods that might destroy the nation
(2) struggling with the arrival of large numbers of freedom-seeking refugees
(3) facing several dangers that threaten its existence as a new nation
(4) celebrating its success as an independent nation

43 One way in which the Tang dynasty, the Gupta Empire, and the European Renaissance are similar is that they all included periods of

(1) religious unity
(2) democratic reforms
(3) economic isolation
(4) cultural achievements

44 What was one similar goal shared by Simón Bolívar and Mohandas Gandhi?

(1) ending foreign control
(2) promoting religious freedom
(3) establishing a limited monarchy
(4) creating collective farms

45 The Armenian Massacre, the "killing fields" of the Khmer Rouge, and Saddam Hussein's attacks against the Kurds are examples of

(1) apartheid
(2) enslavement
(3) human rights violations
(4) forced collectivization

46 In western Europe, the Middle Ages began after the collapse of which empire?

(1) Mughal   (3) Ottoman
(2) Roman   (4) Byzantine

Base your answers to questions 47 and 48 on the chart below and on your knowledge of social studies.

Executions During the Reign of Terror

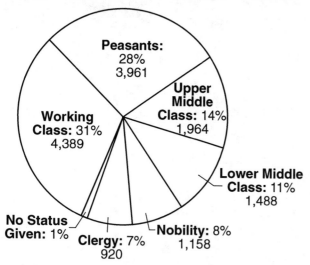

Peasants: 28% 3,961

Upper Middle Class: 14% 1,964

Working Class: 31% 4,389

Lower Middle Class: 11% 1,488

No Status Given: 1%

Clergy: 7% 920

Nobility: 8% 1,158

Source: Dennis Sherman et al., eds., *World Civilizations: Sources, Images, and Interpretations,* McGraw-Hill (adapted)

47 During which revolution did these executions occur?

(1) French
(2) Russian
(3) Chinese
(4) Cuban

48 Which statement is best supported by information found in this chart?

(1) Clergy were spared from the Reign of Terror.
(2) The Reign of Terror affected all classes equally.
(3) The Reign of Terror crossed social and economic boundaries.
(4) Peasants were the most frequent victims of the Reign of Terror.

Base your answer to question 49 on the passage below and on your knowledge of social studies.

. . . Our foundation rests upon trade, because as you see, we have a large part of our capital invested [in it]. And therefore we shall have little for exchange operations, and we are forced to exert our ingenuity elsewhere. This, however, in my opinion, does not involve greater risk than one incurs in exchanges today, especially when no risks at sea are run [That is, when shipments by sea are insured.]; nor does it bring smaller profits. And [trade operations] are more legal and more honorable. In them we shall so govern ourselves that every day you will have more reason to be content; may God grant us His grace. . . .

Source: Letter to the home office of the Medici from branch office at Bruges, May 14, 1464 (adapted)

49 This passage best illustrates circumstances that characterized the

(1) Crusades
(2) Age of Reason
(3) Commercial Revolution
(4) Scientific Revolution

50 "Germany, Austria-Hungary, and Italy Form Triple Alliance"
"Serbian Nationalism Grows in Balkans"
"Archduke Franz Ferdinand Assassinated in Bosnia"

The events in these headlines contributed most directly to the

(1) beginning of World War I
(2) outbreak of the Cold War
(3) development of communist rule in Europe
(4) strengthening of European monarchies

Answers to the essay questions are to be written in the separate essay booklet.

In developing your answer to Part II, be sure to keep these general definitions in mind:

(a) <u>explain</u> means "to make plain or understandable; to give reasons for or causes of; to show the logical development or relationships of"

(b) <u>discuss</u> means "to make observations about something using facts, reasoning, and argument; to present in some detail"

PART II

THEMATIC ESSAY QUESTION

Directions: Write a well-organized essay that includes an introduction, several paragraphs addressing the task below, and a conclusion.

Theme: Movement of People and Goods: Trade

> Trade routes and trade organizations have had an impact on nations and regions. The effects have been both positive and negative.

Task:

> Identify *two* trade routes *and/or* trade organizations and for *each*
> - Explain *one* reason for the establishment of the trade route or trade organization
> - Discuss *one* positive effect *or* *one* negative effect of the trade route or trade organization on a specific nation or region

You may use any example from your study of global history. Some suggestions you might wish to consider include the Silk Roads, the trans-Saharan trade routes of the African kingdoms, Mediterranean trade routes, the Hanseatic League, the British East India Company, the Organization of Petroleum Exporting Countries (OPEC), and the European Union (EU).

You are *not* limited to these suggestions.

Guidelines:

In your essay, be sure to
- Develop all aspects of the task
- Support the theme with relevant facts, examples, and details
- Use a logical and clear plan of organization, including an introduction and a conclusion that are beyond a restatement of the theme

In developing your answer to Part III, be sure to keep this general definition in mind:

> **discuss** means "to make observations about something using facts, reasoning, and argument; to present in some detail"

PART III

DOCUMENT-BASED QUESTION

This question is based on the accompanying documents. It is designed to test your ability to work with historical documents. Some of these documents have been edited for the purposes of this question. As you analyze the documents, take into account the source of each document and any point of view that may be presented in the document.

Historical Context:

> As World War II came to an end, a new conflict emerged between the United States and the Soviet Union. This conflict, known as the Cold War, affected many regions of the world, including **Europe**, **Asia**, and **Latin America**.

Task: Using information from the documents and your knowledge of global history, answer the questions that follow each document in Part A. Your answers to the questions will help you write the Part B essay in which you will be asked to

> • Discuss how the Cold War between the United States and the Soviet Union affected other nations **and/or** regions of the world

Part A
Short-Answer Questions

Directions: Analyze the documents and answer the short-answer questions that follow each document in the space provided.

Document 1

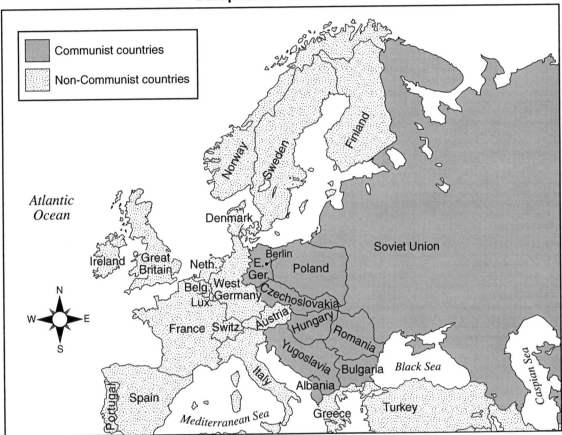

Europe After World War II

Source: Roger B. Beck et al., *World History: Patterns of Interaction*, McDougal Littell (adapted)

1 What does the information shown on this map indicate about the governments of Western Europe and Eastern Europe after World War II? [1]

_____

_____

Score [ ]

Document 2a

Imre Nagy, the Hungarian leader, was forced out of office by the Soviet Communist government. The people of Hungary protested his removal from office.

> This is Hungary calling! This is Hungary calling! The last free station. Forward to the United Nations. Early this morning Soviet troops launched a general attack on Hungary. We are requesting you to send us immediate aid in the form of parachute troops over the Transdanubian provinces [across the Danube River]. It is possible that our broadcasts will soon come to the same fate as the other Hungarian broadcasting stations . . . For the sake of God and freedom, help Hungary! . . .
>
> — Free Radio Rakoczi
>
> Civilized people of the world, listen and come to our aid. Not with declarations, but with force, with soldiers, with arms. Do not forget that there is no stopping the wild onslaught [attack] of Bolshevism. Your turn will also come, if we perish. Save our souls! Save our souls! . . .
>
> — Free Radio Petofi

Source: Melvin J. Lasky, ed., *The Hungarian Revolution: The Story of the October Uprising as Recorded in Documents, Dispatches, Eye-Witness Accounts, and World-wide Reactions*, Frederick A. Praeger, 1957 (adapted)

2a Based on these broadcasts from Free Radio Rakoczi and Free Radio Petofi, state **two** reasons the Hungarian people were asking for help in 1956. [2]

(1) _____

_____

Score ⬤

(2) _____

_____

Score ☐

Document 2b

> This morning the forces of the reactionary conspiracy [anti-Soviet plot] against the Hungarian people were crushed. A new Hungarian Revolutionary Worker-Peasant [Communist] Government, headed by the Prime Minister Janos Kadar, has been formed. . . .
>
> — Radio Moscow

Source: Melvin J. Lasky, ed., *The Hungarian Revolution: The Story of the October Uprising as Recorded in Documents, Dispatches, Eye-Witness Accounts, and World-wide Reactions*, Frederick A. Praeger, 1957

2b Based on this broadcast from Radio Moscow, state **one** result of the Hungarian Revolution. [1]

_____

_____

Score ⬤

Document 3a

Berlin, Germany After World War II

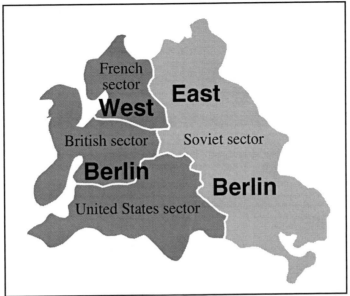

French sector

West

East

British sector

Soviet sector

Berlin

United States sector

Berlin

Source: Henry Brun et al., *Reviewing Global History and Geography,*
AMSCO (adapted)

Document 3b

Berlin, 1961

Source: Heiko Burkhardt, dailysoft.com

3 Based on this map and the Burkhardt photograph, state *one* way the Cold War affected the city of Berlin. [1]

_____

_____

Score ▢

Document 4

. . . The preservation of peace forms the central aim of India's policy. It is in the pursuit of this policy that we have chosen the path of nonalinement [nonalignment] in any military or like pact or alliance. Nonalinement does not mean passivity of mind or action, lack of faith or conviction. It does not mean submission to what we consider evil. It is a positive and dynamic approach to such problems that confront us. We believe that each country has not only the right to freedom but also to decide its own policy and way of life. Only thus can true freedom flourish and a people grow according to their own genius.

We believe, therefore, in nonaggression and noninterference by one country in the affairs of another and the growth of tolerance between them and the capacity for peaceful coexistence. We think that by the free exchange of ideas and trade and other contacts between nations each will learn from the other and truth will prevail. We therefore endeavor to maintain friendly relations with all countries, even though we may disagree with them in their policies or structure of government. We think that by this approach we can serve not only our country but also the larger causes of peace and good fellowship in the world. . . .

Source: Prime Minister Jawaharlal Nehru, speech in Washington, D.C., December 18, 1956

4 According to Prime Minister Nehru, what was India's foreign policy in 1956? [1]

_____

_____

Score ⬜

Document 5

Sook Nyul Choi was born in Pyongyang, Korea and immigrated to the United States during the 1950s. She integrates her autobiographical information into a work of historical fiction set in Korea between the end of World War II and 1950.

> . . . Our freedom and happiness did not last long. In June 1950, war broke out. North Korean and Communist soldiers filled the streets of Seoul, and were soon joined by Chinese Communist troops. Russian tanks came barreling through. In the chaos, many more North Korean refugees made their way to Seoul. Theresa and the other nuns finally escaped, and made their way to our house. They told us that the Russians and Town Reds had found out about Kisa's and Aunt Tiger's other activities. They died as all "traitors" did. They were shot with machine guns, and then hanged in the town square to serve as a lesson to others. We never heard any further news about the sock girls, or about my friend Unhi. I still wonder if they are alive in the North.

Source: Sook Nyul Choi, *Year of Impossible Goodbyes*, Houghton Mifflin Company

5 Based on Sook Nyul Choi's description, state *two* ways the beginning of the Korean War affected the people of Korea. [2]

(1)_____

_____

Score ☐

_____

_____

Score ☐

Document 6a

Document 6b

War in Korea, 1950–1953

War in Vietnam, 1954–1973

Source: Burton F. Beers, *World History: Patterns of Civilization*, Prentice Hall (adapted)

6 Based on the information shown on these maps, state *one* similarity in the way the Cold War affected Korea and Vietnam. [1]

_____

_____

Score ☐

Document 7a

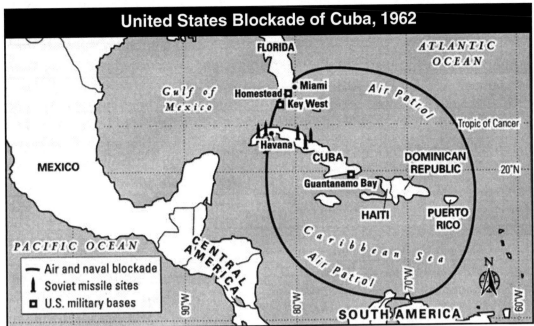

United States Blockade of Cuba, 1962

Source: *World History: Patterns of Interaction*, McDougal Littell (adapted)

Document 7b

This Government as promised has maintained the closest surveillance of the Soviet military build-up on the island of Cuba.

Within the past week unmistakable evidence has established the fact that a series of offensive missile sites is now in preparation on that imprisoned island.

The purpose of these bases can be none other than to provide a nuclear strike capability against the Western Hemisphere.

Upon receiving the first preliminary hard information of this nature last Tuesday morning at 9 A.M., I directed that our surveillance be stepped up. And having now confirmed and completed our evaluation of the evidence and our decision on a course of action, this Government feels obliged to report this new crisis to you in fullest detail.

The characteristics of these new missile sites indicate two distinct types of installations. Several of them include medium-range ballistic missiles capable of carrying a nuclear warhead for a distance of more than 1,000 nautical miles.

Each of these missiles, in short, is capable of striking Washington, D.C., the Panama Canal, Cape Canaveral, Mexico City or any other city in the southeastern part of the United States, in Central America or in the Caribbean area. . . .

Source: President John F. Kennedy, address to the nation on the Soviet arms buildup in Cuba, October 22, 1962

7 Based on this map and President John F. Kennedy's address, state *one* way the Cold War affected Cuba. [1]

_____

_____

Score

Document 8a

. . . Immediately after the revolution, the Sandinistas had the best organized and most experienced military force in the country. To replace the National Guard, the Sandinistas established a new national army, the Sandinista People's Army (Ejército Popular Sandinista—EPS), and a police force, the Sandinista Police (Policía Sandinista-PS). These two groups, contrary to the original Puntarenas Pact [agreement reached by Sandinista government when in exile] were controlled by the Sandinistas and trained by personnel from Cuba, Eastern Europe, and the Soviet Union. Opposition to the overwhelming FSLN [Sandinista National Liberation Front] influence in the security forces did not surface until 1980. Meanwhile, the EPS developed, with support from Cuba and the Soviet Union, into the largest and best equipped military force in Central America. Compulsory military service, introduced during 1983, brought the EPS forces to about 80,000 by the mid-1980s. . . .

Source: Library of Congress, Federal Research Division (adapted)

8a According to this document from the Library of Congress, what effect did the Cold War have on Nicaragua in the 1980s? [1]

_____

_____

Score ☐

Document 8b

Her [Violeta Chamorro] husband's murder sparked a revolution that brought the Sandinistas to power w Violeta Chamorro is challenging them in Nicaragua's presidential election.

. . . "Violeta! Violeta! Throw them [Sandinistas] out! Throw them out!"

Surrounded by outstretched hands, Mrs. Chamorro hugs everyone in reach. Then Nicaragua's most famous widow goes straight to her message. This is the town where my husband was born, she tells them. This is where he learned the values of freedom that cost him his life. This is where he would tell us to make a stand against the Sandinista regime.

"I never thought that I would return to Granada as a candidate, raising the banner steeped in the blood of Pedro Joaquín Chamorro, to ask his people once again to put themselves in the front lines," she says. "But Nicaragua must win its freedom once again.

"All across the world," she continues, her voice rising, "people like you are burying Communism and proclaiming democracy. So set your watches! Set them to the same hour as Poland, as Bulgaria, as Czechoslovakia, as Chile! Because this is the hour of democracy and freedom — this is the hour of the people!". . .

Source: Mark A. Uhlig, *New York Times*, February 11, 1990

8b According to Mark A. Uhlig, what political change did Violeta Chamorro hope to bring to Nicaragua? [1]

_____

_____

Score ☐

Part B

Essay

Directions: Write a well-organized essay that includes an introduction, several paragraphs, and a conclusion. Use evidence from *at least **five*** documents to support your response. Support your response with relevant facts, examples, and details. Include additional outside information.

Historical Context:

As World War II came to an end, a new conflict emerged between the United States and the Soviet Union. This conflict, known as the Cold War, affected many regions of the world, including **Europe**, **Asia**, and **Latin America**.

Task: Using the information from the documents and your knowledge of global history, write an essay in which you

> • Discuss how the Cold War between the United States and the Soviet Union affected other nations ***and/or*** regions of the world

Guidelines:

In your essay, be sure to
- Develop all aspects of the task
- Incorporate information from *at least **five*** documents
- Incorporate relevant outside information
- Support the theme with relevant facts, examples, and details
- Use a logical and clear plan of organization, including an introduction and a conclusion that are beyond a restatement of the theme

The University of the State of New York

GLOBAL HISTORY AND GEOGRAPHY

Wednesday, August 16, 2006 — 12:30 to 3:30 p.m., only

ANSWER SHEET

Sex: ☐ Male ☐ Female

Student ....

Teacher ....

School ....

Write your answers for Part I on this answer sheet, write your answers to Part III A in the test booklet, and write your answers for Parts II and III B in the separate essay booklet.

FOR TEACHER USE ONLY

Part I Score _____

Part III A Score _____

Total Part I and III A Score [ ]

Part II Essay Score _____

Part III B Essay Score _____

Total Essay Score [ ]

Final Score
(obtained from conversion chart) [ ]

Part I

1.........	26.........
2.........	27.........
3.........	28.........
4.........	29.........
5.........	30.........
6.........	31.........
7.........	32.........
8.........	33.........
9.........	34.........
10.........	35.........
11.........	36.........
12.........	37.........
13.........	38.........
14.........	39.........
15.........	40.........
16.........	41.........
17.........	42.........
18.........	43.........
19.........	44.........
20.........	45.........
21.........	46.........
22.........	47.........
23.........	48.........
24.........	49.........
25.........	50.........

No. Right [ ]

The declaration below should be signed when you have completed the examination.

I hereby affirm, at the close of this examination, that I had no unlawful knowledge of the questions or answers prior to the examination and that I have neither given nor received assistance in answering any of the questions during the examination.

_____

Signature

REGENTS IN GLOBAL HISTORY AND GEOGRAPHY

Tear Here